ORIGO
STEPPING STONES
2.0
COMPREHENSIVE MATHEMATICS

AUTHORS

James Burnett
Calvin Irons
Peter Stowasser
Allan Turton

PROGRAM CONSULTANTS

Diana Lambdin
Frank Lester, Jr.
Kit Norris

CONTRIBUTING WRITER

Beth Lewis

STUDENT BOOK B

ORIGO
EDUCATION

CONTENTS

CONTENTS

© ORIGO Education

ORIGO Stepping Stones • Grade 2

Step In Look at the counter on this number chart.

How would you move the counter to show a number that is 2 less?

How would you move the counter to show a number that is 10 less?

How would you move the counter to show a number that is 12 less?

11	12	13	14	15	16	17	18	19	20
21	22	23	24	25	26	27	28	29	30
31	32	33	34	35	36	37	38	39	40
41	42	43	44	45	46	(47)	48	49	50
51	52	53	54	55	56	57	58	59	60

I would start at 47 and subtract the tens then the ones. 47 take away 10 is 37. Then 2 less is 35.

I subtracted the ones first. 47 take away 2 is 45. Then 10 less is 35.

Complete each of these equations. Draw arrows on the chart above to help your thinking.

16 – 1 = 10

39 – 20 = 20

55 – 3 = 3

35 – 21 = 21

Step Up 1. Draw arrows on the chart above to show how you figure out each of these. Then write the differences.

a. 34 – 2 = 1

b. 43 – 10 = 2

c. 50 – 1 = 17

d. 15 – 3 = 18

e. 55 – 30 = 17

f. 32 – 20 = 19

g. 25 – 12 = 88

h. 50 – 21 = 19

i. 48 – 23 = 91

2. Write the differences. Use the number chart to help.

a.

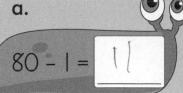

80 − 1 = 11

51	52	53	54	55	56	57	58	59	60
61	62	63	64	65	66	67	68	69	70
71	72	73	74	75	76	77	78	79	80
81	82	83	84	85	86	87	88	89	90
91	92	93	94	95	96	97	98	99	100

b.

90 − 20 = 18

c.

63 − 11 = 11

d.

75 − 3 = 19

e.

79 − 21 = 11

f.

60 − 2 = 18

g.

85 − 13 = 17

h.

90 − 31 = 16

3. Figure out and write the differences.

a.

53 − 10 = 6

b.

68 − 30 = 17

c.

47 − 2 = 15

d.

65 − 21 = 19

e.

25 − 10 = 19

f.

30 − 13 = 16

Step Ahead   Write the missing numbers along the trail.

98 → −12 → 11 → −21 → 98 → −23 → 79 → −11 → 9

Step In

How much will be left in the wallet after buying the cap?

$57 $13

How do you know?

Use this number line to show how you figured it out.

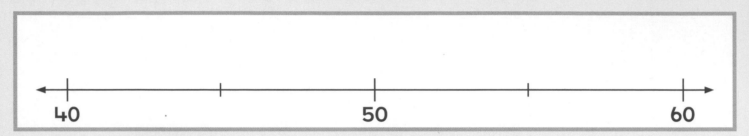

40   50   60

I started at 57 and counted back the tens then the ones of the price. I can draw jumps like this to show how I subtracted.

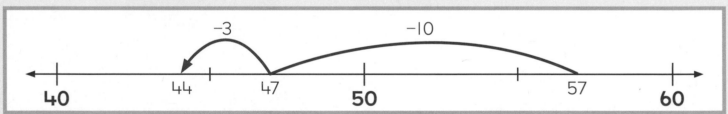

−3   −10

40   44   47   50   57   60

Step Up

1. a. Draw jumps on this number line to show how you would figure out 68 − 12.

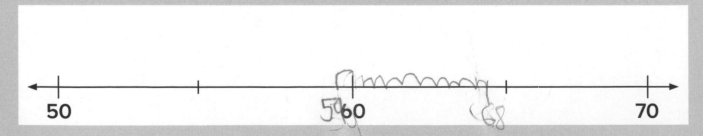

50   50 60   68   70

b. Draw jumps to show another way you could figure out 68 − 12.

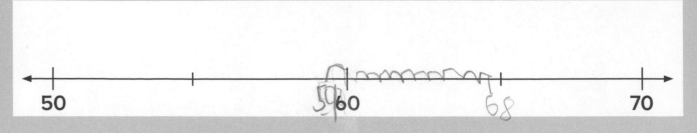

50   50 60   68   70

2. Complete each sentence. Draw jumps on the number line to show your thinking.

a.

66 – 13 = 57

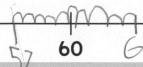

```
+----------+----------+----------+----------+----------+----------+
40         50              57   60   66              70
```

b.

57 – 15 = 47

```
+----------+----------+----------+----------+----------+
30              40         47   50              57,7    60
```

c.

85 – 21 = 66

```
+----------+----------+----------+----------+----------+----------+
60         66    70              80   85              90
```

d.

67 – 23 = ☐

```
+----------+----------+----------+----------+----------+----------+
40         44         50              60         67    70
```

Step Ahead   Draw a number line to help you figure out the difference.

79 – 25 = 60

ORIGO Stepping Stones · Grade 2 · 7.2

Computation Practice   What goes up and never comes down?

★ Write the totals. Then color the part below that matches each total.

35 + 35 = ____   25 + 25 = ____   45 + 45 = ____   20 + 20 = ____

30 + 30 = ____   15 + 15 = ____   40 + 40 = ____

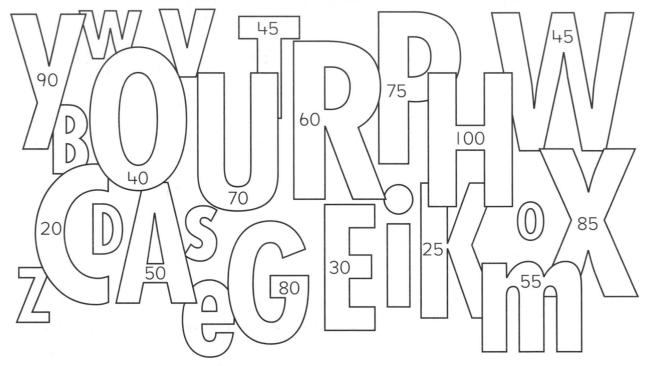

Write these totals as fast as you can.

30 + 31 = ____   20 + 21 = ____   10 + 11 = ____

40 + 41 = ____   15 + 16 = ____   35 + 36 = ____

25 + 26 = ____   45 + 46 = ____   16 + 17 = ____

Ongoing Practice

1. Write the totals.

a. $22 + 22 = \boxed{}$

b. $12 + 12 = \boxed{}$

c. $33 + 33 = \boxed{}$

d. $42 + 42 = \boxed{}$

e. $23 + 23 = \boxed{}$

f. $31 + 31 = \boxed{}$

2. Write the differences. Use the number chart to help.

a. $84 - 20 = \underline{}$

b. $93 - 2 = \underline{}$

c. $91 - 30 = \underline{}$

d. $80 - 3 = \underline{}$

51	52	53	54	55	56	57	58	59	60
61	62	63	64	65	66	67	68	69	70
71	72	73	74	75	76	77	78	79	80
81	82	83	84	85	86	87	88	89	90
91	92	93	94	95	96	97	98	99	100

Preparing for Module 8

Figure out how much **more** money is needed to pay the price. Draw jumps to show your thinking.

a.

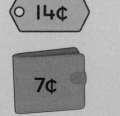

14¢

7¢

4	5	6	7	8	9	10	11	12	13	14

Amount needed is $\boxed{}$ ¢

b.

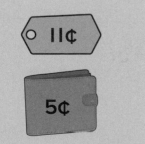

11¢

5¢

4	5	6	7	8	9	10	11	12	13	14

Amount needed is $\boxed{}$ ¢

Step In How can you show each equation on the number chart?

7 – 5 = ____

17 – 5 = ____

27 – 5 = ____

37 – 5 = ____

47 – 5 = ____

Color each starting number blue, and each difference red. What patterns do you see?

1	2	3	4	5	6	7	8	9	10
11	12	13	14	15	16	17	18	19	20
21	22	23	24	25	26	27	28	29	30
31	32	33	34	35	36	37	38	39	40
41	42	43	44	45	46	47	48	49	50

This number line shows how to use ten to help subtract.

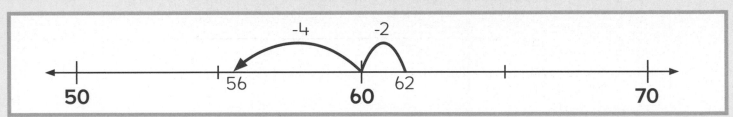

What equation is being shown? How do you know?
Which ten is being used? Why is that number helpful?

Step Up 1. Use patterns to help you complete each equation.

a.
12 – 4 = ____

22 – 4 = ____

32 – 4 = ____

52 – 4 = ____

b.
14 – 8 = ____

24 – 8 = ____

34 – 8 = ____

64 – 8 = ____

c.
15 – 7 = ____

25 – 7 = ____

35 – 7 = ____

55 – 7 = ____

2. Complete each equation. Draw jumps on the number line to show your thinking.

a.

$55 - 6 =$ ☐

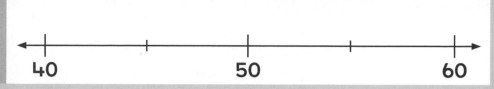

b.

$74 - 8 =$ ☐

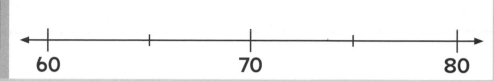

c.

$41 - 7 =$ ☐

d.

$62 - 9 =$ ☐

e.

$85 - 6 =$ ☐

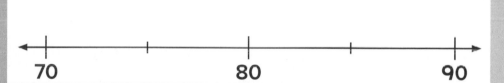

Step Ahead	Solve the problem. Draw jumps on the number line to show your thinking.

Owen has 72 football cards in his collection. There are 150 different cards to collect. Owen gives 9 cards to his sister. How many football cards does Owen have left? ☐ cards

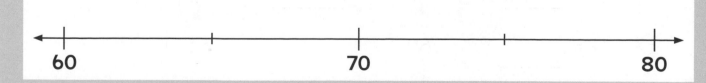

Step In   Imagine you have $53.

Which item would you like to buy?

 $16    $38

How much money will you have left? How do you know?

I could start at
$53 and subtract
$38 like this.

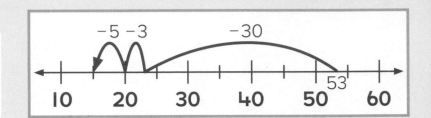

How would you subtract $16 from $53?

Show your thinking on this
number line.

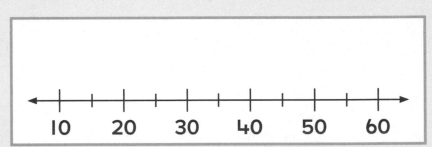

Step Up   1.   Figure out the **difference**. Draw jumps on the number line
to show your thinking. Then complete the equation.

a.

$45 – $22 = $_____

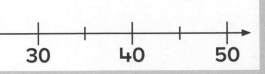

b.

$48 – $15 = $_____

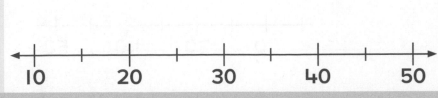

2. Figure out the **difference**. Draw jumps to show your thinking. Then complete the subtraction equation.

a.

$54 - 18 = \boxed{}$

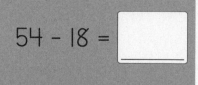

b.

$63 - 37 = \boxed{}$

c.

$65 - 26 = \boxed{}$

d.

$52 - 27 = \boxed{}$

Step Ahead Gabriel bought a new soccer ball. He gave the salesperson $55 and received $17 in change. How much did the ball cost?

a. Draw jumps on this number line to show how you figure out the price of the ball.

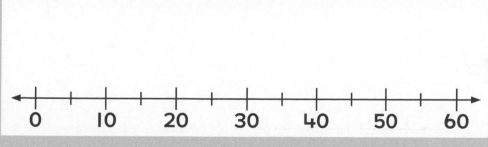

b. Write the cost of the soccer ball on the price tag.

Think and Solve Cross out one number from one box, and write it below another box so that the total of each box of numbers equals 40.

6	15	10

[ ]

9	14	26

[ ]

9	18	13

[ ]

Words at Work

Write about subtracting on a hundred chart.
You can use words from the list to help you.

up	back	left	right
down	across	tens	ones
subtract	move	count back	

1	2	3	4	5	6	7	8	9	10
11	12	13	14	15	16	17	18	19	20
21	22	23	24	25	26	27	28	29	30
31	32	33	34	35	36	37	38	39	40
41	42	43	44	45	46	47	48	49	50
51	52	53	54	55	56	57	58	59	60
61	62	63	64	65	66	67	68	69	70
71	72	73	74	75	76	77	78	79	80
81	82	83	84	85	86	87	88	89	90
91	92	93	94	95	96	97	98	99	100

Ongoing Practice

1. Complete each equation. Show your thinking.

a.

38 + 45 = ☐

b.

27 + 19 = ☐

2. Use patterns to help you complete each sentence.

a.
11 – 5 = ☐

21 – 5 = ☐

31 – 5 = ☐

41 – 5 = ☐

b.
15 – 9 = ☐

25 – 9 = ☐

35 – 9 = ☐

45 – 9 = ☐

c.
13 – 8 = ☐

23 – 8 = ☐

33 – 8 = ☐

43 – 8 = ☐

Preparing for Module 8

Add the tens blocks then add the ones blocks. Write the total value of the blocks.

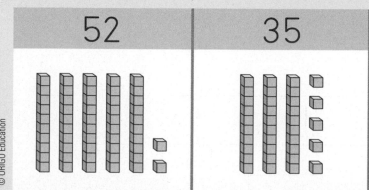

52

35

There are ☐ tens.

There are ☐ ones.

☐ and ☐ is ☐

Step In

Imagine you had $52.
Which item can you buy?

How much money will you have left?
How do you know?

What equation would you
write to show the difference?

How could you use addition to figure out the amount that is left over?

I could start at $45 and count on to $52 on the
number line below. I could then add the jumps
that I made to figure out the amount left over.

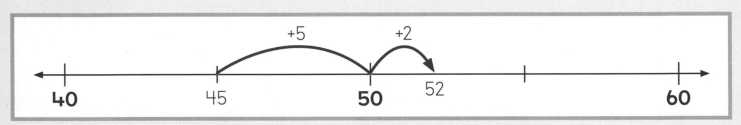

How much more money do you need to buy the bicycle?

What subtraction problem could you write?

How would you figure out the difference? Explain your thinking.

Step Up

1. Draw jumps to show how you could **count on** to find
the difference. Then write the difference.

$57 - 40 = \boxed{}$

2. Use addition to figure out the difference. Draw jumps to show your thinking.

a.
$68 - 49 = \boxed{}$

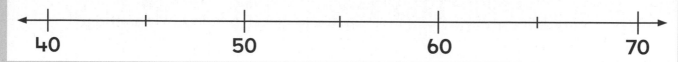

b.
$55 - 38 = \boxed{}$

c.
$51 - 36 = \boxed{}$

d.
$62 - 45 = \boxed{}$

Step Ahead

Tama has $45. He wants to buy two games that cost $32 and $35. How much more money does he need to save?

$_____

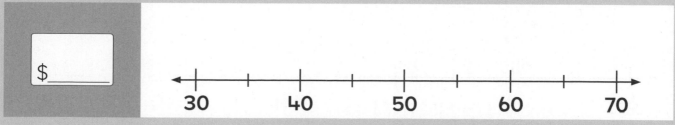

© ORIGO Education

Step In

These two older students measured the length of their long jumps.

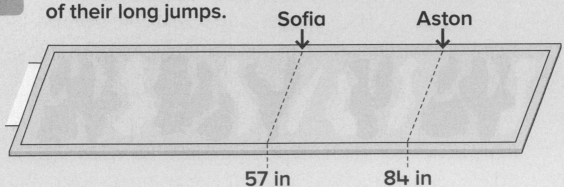

Sofia   Aston

57 in   84 in

What is the length of each student's long jump?

How could you figure out the difference between the lengths of their jumps?

I could start at 57 and count on to 84 like this.

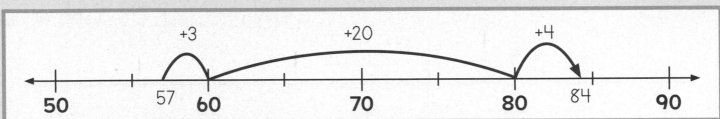

How could you count on in just two steps?

What equation could you write to show the difference?

Step Up

1. Alisa's jump was 53 inches and Allan's jump was 75 inches. Count on to figure out the difference. Draw jumps to show your thinking. Then complete the equation.

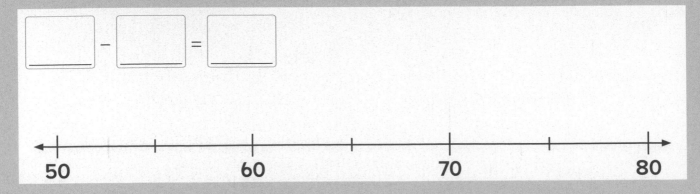

☐ − ☐ = ☐

2. These students measured their long jumps. Count on to figure out the difference between the lengths of these students' jumps. Then write the equation to show the difference. Draw jumps to show your thinking.

Student	Jump
Jude	58 in
Bella	74 in
Archie	71 in
Bianca	54 in

a. Bella's jump and Jude's jump

50   60   70   80

b. Archie's jump and Bianca's jump

50   60   70   80

c. Jude's jump and Archie's jump

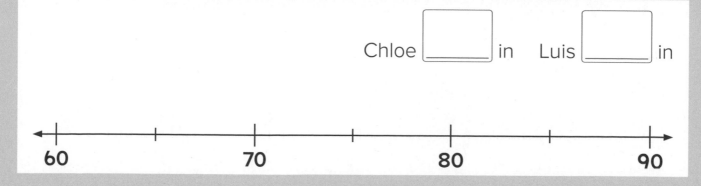

Step Ahead

Franco's jump was 85 inches. This was 21 inches more than Chloe's and 5 inches less than Luis's. Use the number line to figure out the length of each jump.

Chloe [____] in   Luis [____] in

60   70   80   90

Computation Practice

★ Write the differences as fast as you can.

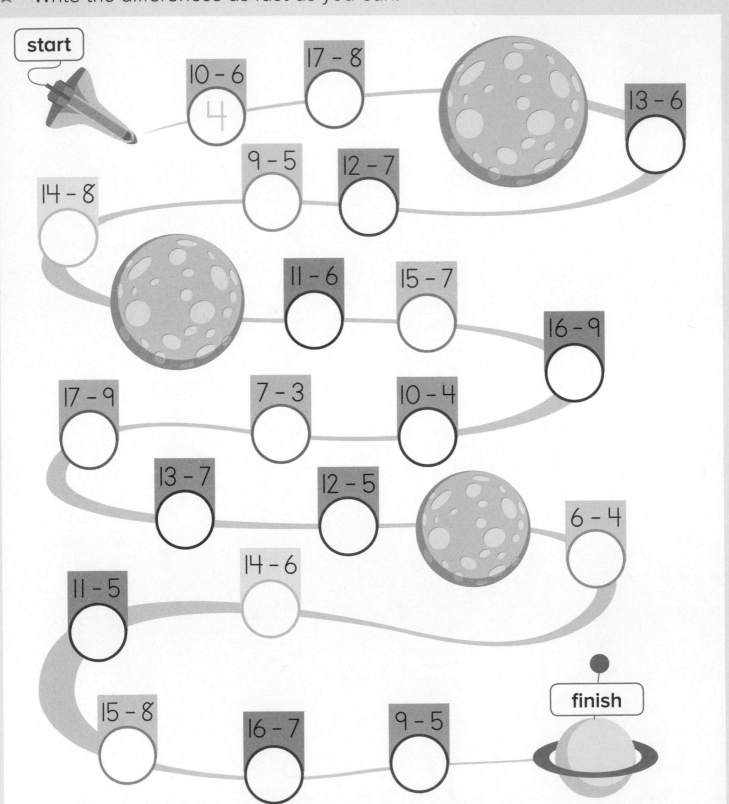

start

10 − 6
4

17 − 8

13 − 6

9 − 5

12 − 7

14 − 8

11 − 6

15 − 7

16 − 9

17 − 9

7 − 3

10 − 4

13 − 7

12 − 5

6 − 4

14 − 6

11 − 5

finish

15 − 8

16 − 7

9 − 5

I. Estimate each total. Color the cards that have a total greater than 70.

a. 32 + 17	**b.** 64 + 27	**c.** 12 + 61	**d.** 48 + 13
e. 22 + 53	**f.** 27 + 59	**g.** 26 + 29	**h.** 12 + 53

FROM 2.6.5

2. Draw jumps to show how you could **count on** to find the difference. Then write the difference.

a.

65 – 37 = ☐

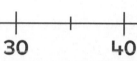
30   40   50   60   70

b.

75 – 48 = ☐

40   50   60   70   80

FROM 2.7.5

Preparing for Module 8

Add the tens then the ones. Write an equation to match.

a.

28	35	☐ + ☐ = ☐

b.

19	42	☐ + ☐ = ☐

Step In   Look at the prices of these original paintings.

Which painting costs more?

How much more does the cat painting cost than the painting of the dog?

Kay figures out the difference on a number line.

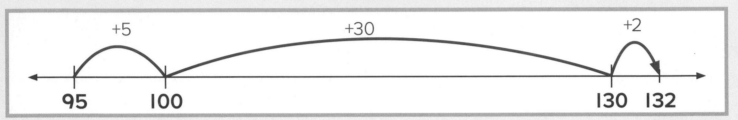

What steps does Kay follow?

What is the difference?
What equation would you write?

If counting on to figure out the difference, you have to add the jumps you make.

Why is it sometimes helpful to make a jump to 100?

Step Up   1.   Draw jumps on the number line to figure out the difference. Try jumping to 100 to help your thinking.

a.

120 − 30 = ____

100

b.

126 − 50 = ____

100

2. Draw jumps on the number line to figure out the difference. Try jumping to 100 to help your thinking.

a.

130 – 75 = ☐

← ─────────────┼───────────── →
              100

b.

115 – 83 = ☐

← ─────────────┼───────────── →
              100

c.

105 – 67 = ☐

← ─────────────┼───────────── →
              100

3. Draw jumps to figure out each difference.

a.

130 – 86 = ☐

← ───────────────────────── →

a.

127 – 92 = ☐

← ───────────────────────── →

Step Ahead   Solve this problem. Draw jumps on the number line to show your thinking.

120 movie tickets were sold in total. 68 tickets were sold on the website. The rest were sold at the booth. How many tickets were sold at the booth?

← ───────────────────────── →   ☐ tickets

Step In   This poster shows the cost of tickets to a concert. Some seats are closer to the stage, so they cost more.

What is the difference in cost between the Gold and General tickets? How do you know?

Two friends share their strategies.

Lifen uses a number line.

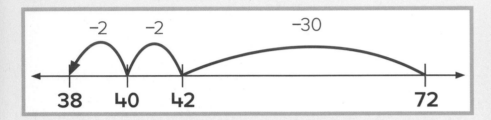

What is similar about the two strategies?

Jayden uses a written method. He subtracts the tens then the ones.

$$72 - 30 = 42$$
$$42 - 4 = 38$$

What steps does Jayden follow?

Use Jayden's strategy to figure out the difference in cost between the Gold and Silver tickets.

I would count on to figure out the difference.

$$55 + ⑮ = 70$$
$$70 + ② = 72$$

$$15 + 2 = 17$$

Step Up   I.   Use the ticket prices at the top of the page to solve this problem. Show your thinking.

Victoria has $150 in her purse. She buys one Silver ticket. How much money does she have left?

$_____

© ORIGO Education

2. Solve each problem. Show your thinking.

a. The band is asked to play for 90 minutes. They have already played for 35 minutes. How many more minutes should they play?

 _____ minutes

b. 45 people are seated in one row. Some of the people leave. There are now 28 people seated in that row. How many people have left?

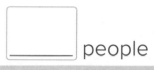 _____ people

c. 42 people are on a bus. 10 people get off at Stop 1, and 12 more people get off at Stop 2. How many people are still on the bus?

 _____ people

d. Concert tickets are being sold at the booth. 52 tickets have been sold. 90 tickets are left. How many tickets were there at the start?

_____ tickets

Step Ahead Read the problem. Then circle the thinking that you could use to solve it. There is more than one way of thinking.

Anya's ticket costs $25 more than Paul's ticket. Anya pays $79 for her ticket and she has $10 left over. How much did Paul pay for his ticket?

a. $69 - 25 =$ ☐

b. $25 +$ ☐ $= 79$

c. $79 - 25 =$ ☐

Think and Solve This map shows a bus route. Trace over the lines in red to show the **shortest** trip between Springfield and Bald Hills. Write the total time.

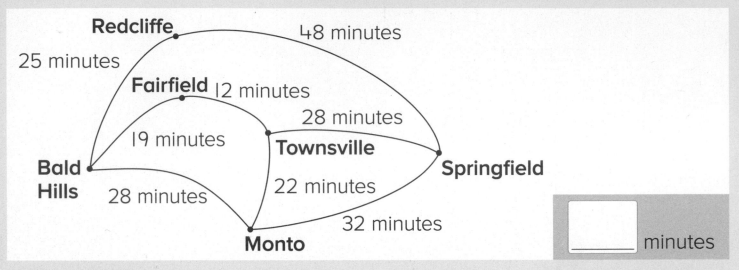

Redcliffe
48 minutes
25 minutes
Fairfield 12 minutes
28 minutes
19 minutes
Townsville
Bald Hills
Springfield
28 minutes
22 minutes
32 minutes
Monto

☐ minutes

Words at Work Write about two different ways you can figure out the difference between 75 and 58. You can use words from the list to help you.

count on

subtract

tens

ones

hundred chart

count back

1. Complete each equation. You can use blocks or make notes on page 280 to help.

a.
42 + 60 = ☐

b.
71 + 40 = ☐

c.
28 + 90 = ☐

FROM 2.6.7

d.
37 + 80 = ☐

e.
50 + 73 = ☐

f.
70 + 47 = ☐

2. Draw jumps on the number line to figure out the difference.
Try jumping to 100 to help your thinking.

a.
120 − 65 = ☐

100

FROM 2.7.7

b.
105 − 37 = ☐

100

Preparing for Module 8   For each number, write the **ten** that is closest.

60   70   80

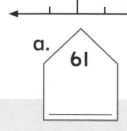
a.
61
___

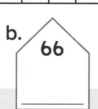
b.
66
___

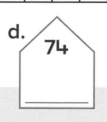
c.
72
___

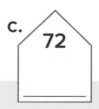
d.
74
___

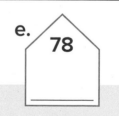
e.
78
___

80   90   100

f.
83
___

g.
87
___

h.
92
___

i.
97
___

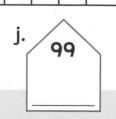
j.
99
___

Step In   What do you know about these shapes?

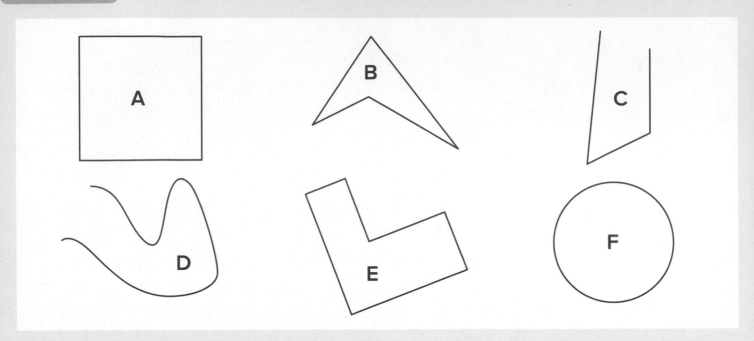

Which of these 2D shapes are open? Which are closed?
Circle the **closed** shapes.

Look at the closed shapes. Which shapes have straight sides?

2D shapes that are closed **and** have all straight sides are **polygons**.
Each shape might have another name, like the square, but they are
all types of polygons.

Step Up   1.   Inside each polygon, write the number of sides.

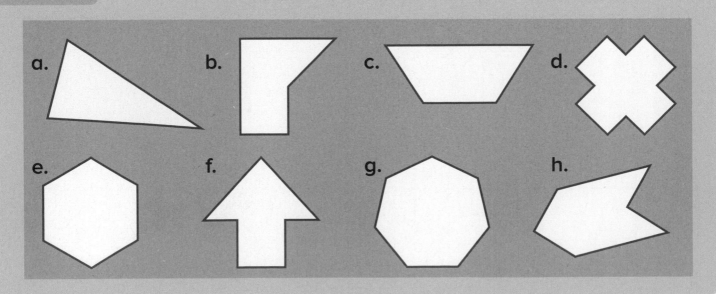

2. Color the polygons.

a.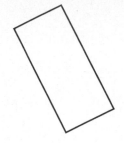

b.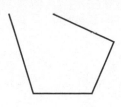

c.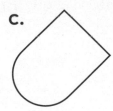

d.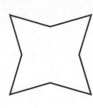

e.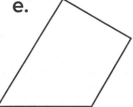

f.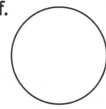

g.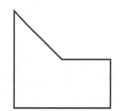

h.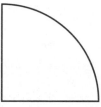

i.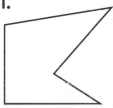

j.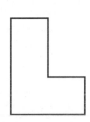

k.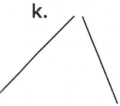

l.

Step Ahead	Color the polygons you find in the pictures below. Write **N** inside the shapes that are **not** polygons.

a.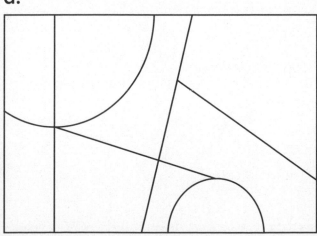

b.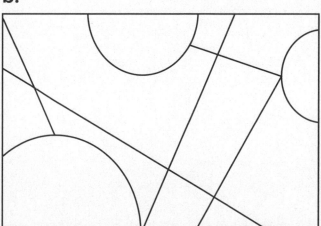

Step In   Look at these shapes. What is the same about them?

What is different?

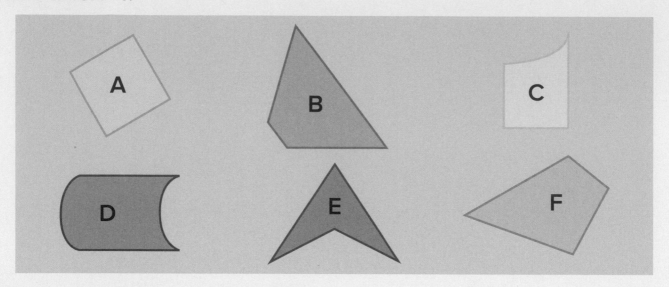

Which of the shapes are polygons?

How do you know?

Polygons that have exactly four sides are called **quadrilaterals**.

The **quad** part of the word quadrilateral means **four**. The **lateral** part means **side**.

Step Up   1.   Color the quadrilaterals.

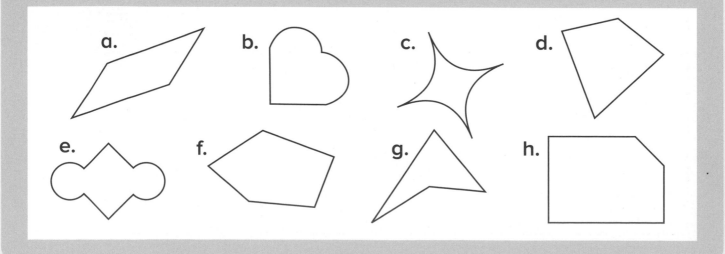

2. Use your ruler to draw more straight sides to make quadrilaterals.

a.
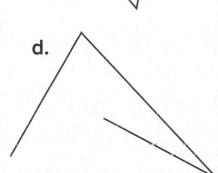

b.

c.
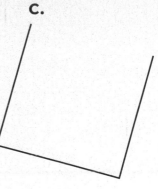

d.

e.
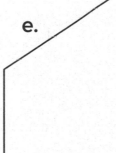

f.
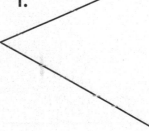

Step Ahead

Color the quadrilaterals you find in the pictures below. Write **N** inside the shapes that are **not** quadrilaterals.

a.

b.

c.
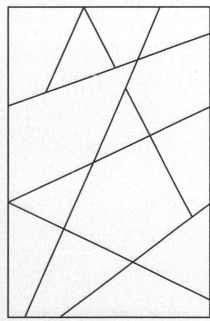

Computation Practice What must you never do in a submarine?

★ Complete the equations. Then write each letter above its matching total at the bottom of the page.

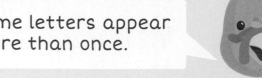
Some letters appear more than once.

15 + 16 = ☐ **f**

14 + 14 = ☐ **i**

22 + 23 = ☐ **n**

41 + 39 = ☐ **r**

19 + 19 = ☐ **p**

12 + 13 = ☐ **d**

26 + 25 = ☐ **s**

29 + 29 = ☐ **h**

35 + 34 = ☐ **o**

45 + 46 = ☐ **a**

31 + 32 = ☐ **e**

41 + 43 = ☐ **w**

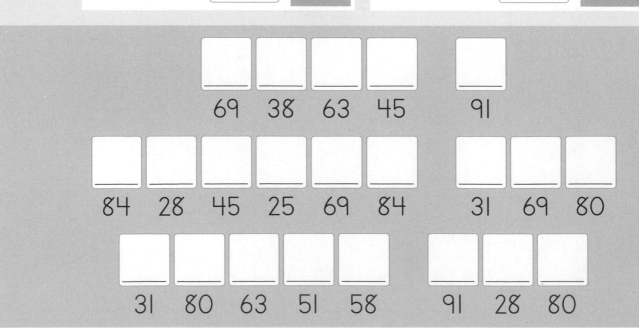

☐ ☐ ☐ ☐   ☐
69 38 63 45   91

☐ ☐ ☐ ☐ ☐ ☐   ☐ ☐ ☐
84 28 45 25 69 84   31 69 80

☐ ☐ ☐ ☐ ☐   ☐ ☐ ☐
31 80 63 51 58   91 28 80

1. Look at this graph.

Favorite Fruit Juice						⊔ means 1 vote	
Apple	⊔	⊔	⊔				
Grape	⊔	⊔	⊔	⊔	⊔	⊔	
Orange	⊔	⊔	⊔	⊔			

a. Which fruit juice is most popular? _____

b. How many more students voted for the most popular juice than the least popular juice? ☐ students

c. How many students voted in total? ☐ students

2. Color the polygons you find in this picture.

   Write **N** inside the shapes that are **not** polygons.

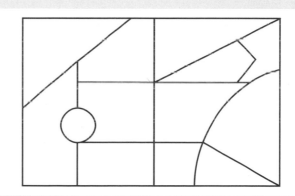

Write the matching time on the digital clock.

a.

b.

c.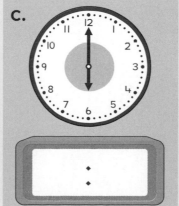

d.

Step In **What do you know about polygons?**

Polygons are closed 2D shapes that have only straight sides. Each polygon has the same number of sides as it has vertices.

What are some shapes that you know are polygons?

There are many other types of polygons.

A **pentagon** is any polygon that has five sides. What do you think **penta** means?

A **hexagon** is any polygon that has six sides. What do you think **hexa** means?

> The poly part of the word polygon means many. The gon part means corner.

Step Up 1. Write **5** inside the pentagons. Write **6** inside the hexagons.

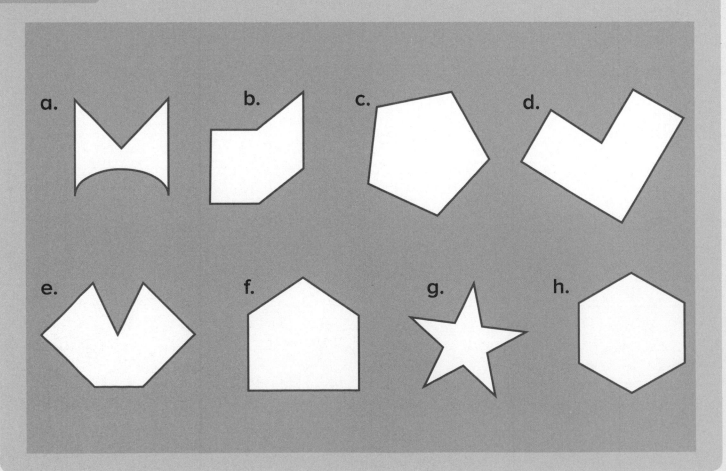

2. Use your ruler to draw lines between vertices to split each shape into triangles. Use as few lines as possible.

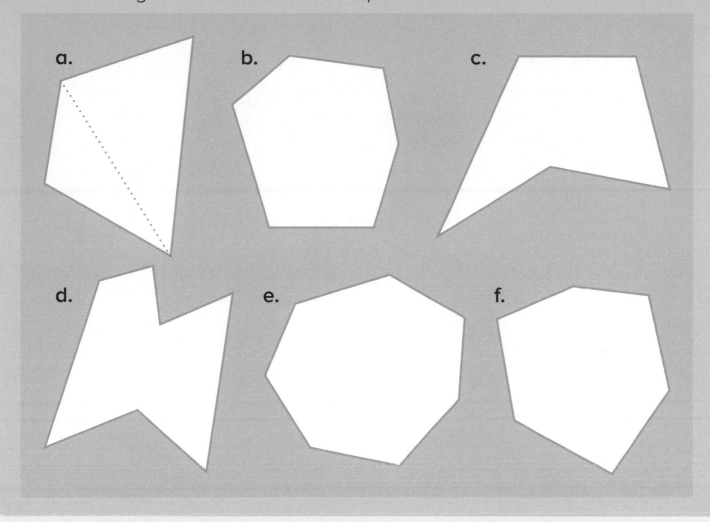

a.

b.

c.

d.

e.

f.

Step Ahead

Use your ruler to draw one line to split each shape into polygons to match the label. Draw lightly until you are sure of your answer.

a. two triangles	b. two quadrilaterals	c. one triangle and one pentagon

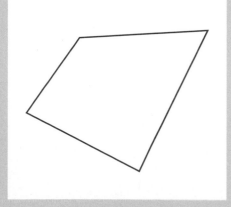

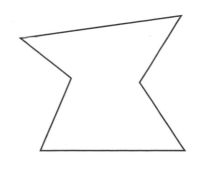

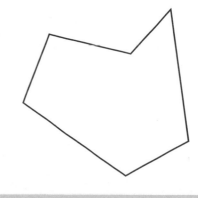

Step In

I am thinking of a 2D shape that is a quadrilateral. It has at least two sides the same length.

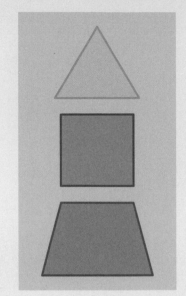

What shape could this be? How do you know?

Draw another quadrilateral that matches the clues.

Then draw a shape that does not match.

Step Up   Draw a shape to match each label.

a. a triangle with exactly two sides the same length

b. a rectangle with all sides the same length

c. a pentagon with all sides a different length

d. a four-sided shape with all sides a different length

e. a hexagon with exactly two sides the same length

f. a quadrilateral with two long sides and two short sides

Step Ahead

a. Write some clues like those above to describe a 2D shape.

b. Exchange clues with another student and draw a shape to match.

Think and Solve Write these numbers in the story below so that it makes sense. Each number can be used only once.

40   2   10   5

Susan has [ ] pet rabbits. She brushes each rabbit for [ ] minutes every afternoon. That takes her [ ] minutes in total. Then she plays with them for [ ] minutes more.

Words at Work   Write the answer for each clue in the grid. Use words from the list.

Clues Across

1. A polygon has the ___ number of sides and vertices.

4. Quadrilaterals have ___ straight sides.

5. Pentagons have ___ straight sides.

6. A ___ is a type of polygon.

Clues Down

1. A polygon has no curved ___.

2. Triangles have ___ straight sides.

3. Hexagons have ___ straight sides.

sides
square
four
five
six
three
same

© ORIGO Education

Ongoing Practice

1. Color the bar graph to match the height of each dog.

   The Bulldog is 7 bricks tall.

   The Pug is 3 bricks tall.

   The Poodle is 5 bricks tall.

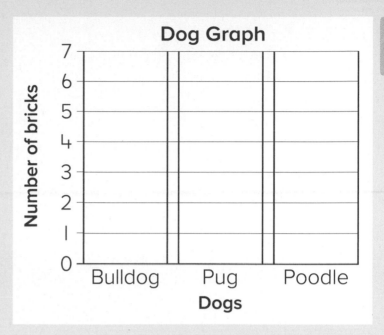

Dog Graph

Number of bricks — Bulldog, Pug, Poodle — Dogs

2. Use your ruler to draw lines between vertices to split each shape into triangles. Use as few lines as possible.

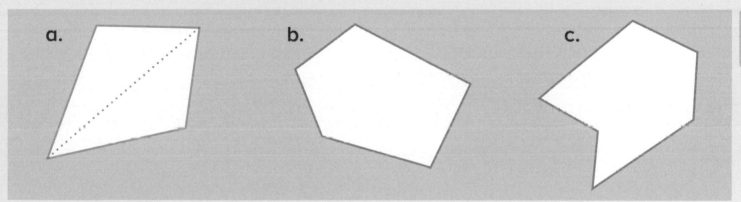

a.　　　　　b.　　　　　c.

Preparing for Module 8

Draw hands on the analog clock to show the matching time.

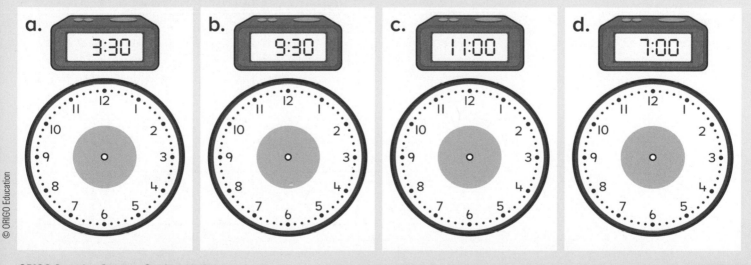

a. 3:30　　b. 9:30　　c. 11:00　　d. 7:00

Step In   Look at these pictures of blocks.

What number does each picture show?

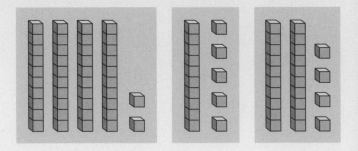

Imagine all the blocks were used to show one number.

How could you figure out what number they would show?

I could add the tens then the ones. There are 7 tens and 11 ones.

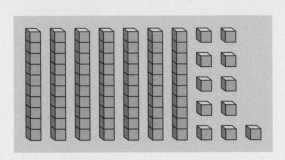

Imagine the total was split into two groups.

What numbers could be in each group? How do you know?

Step Up   1.   Write the number of tens and ones. Then write the total.

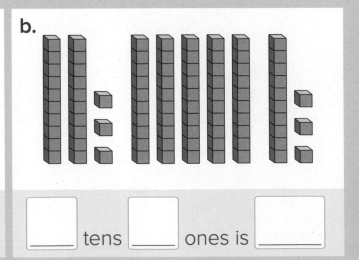

a.

___6___ tens ___7___ ones is ___67___

b.

_____ tens _____ ones is _____

2. Write the number of tens and ones. Then write the total.

a.

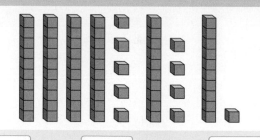

☐ tens ☐ ones is ☐

b.

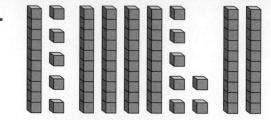

☐ tens ☐ ones is ☐

3. Draw blocks to match.

a. Show 40 split into two parts. One part should show 25.	**b.** Show 50 split into two parts. One part should show 32.

c. Show 70 split into two parts. One part should show 46.	**d.** Show 60 split into two parts. One part should show 37.

Step Ahead   Color some blocks to show three groups. Then write an equation to match.

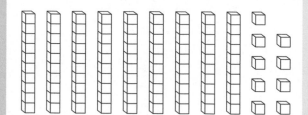

☐ + ☐ + ☐ = ☐

Step In   There are 45 passengers on the bus.

13 passengers get off the bus.
How many passengers are left on the bus?

How can you tell if this problem is about addition or subtraction?

What equation would you write?   45 – 13 = ▢

Henry uses blocks to figure out the difference.

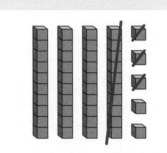

> The answer or unknown part in a subtraction equation is called the **difference**.

What steps does Henry follow?

How does the picture tell you how many passengers are left on the bus?

Step Up   1.   Write the number of tens and ones that are left. You can cross out blocks to help. Then write the difference.

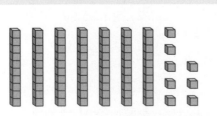

78 – 25 = ▢

There are ▢ 5 ▢ tens.

There are ▢ 3 ▢ ones.

▢ 50 ▢ and ▢ 3 ▢ is ▢ 53 ▢

2. Complete each equation. You can cross out blocks to help.

a.

$59 - 14 = \boxed{}$

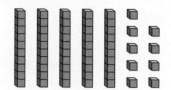

There are _____ tens.

There are _____ ones.

_____ and _____ is _____

b.

$74 - 24 = \boxed{}$

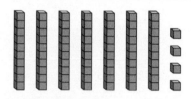

There are _____ tens.

There are _____ ones.

_____ and _____ is _____

c.

$65 - 33 = \boxed{}$

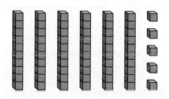

There are _____ tens.

There are _____ ones.

_____ and _____ is _____

3. Complete each equation. You can make notes on page 318 to help.

a. $36 - 15 = \boxed{}$ **b.** $57 - 41 = \boxed{}$ **c.** $68 - 38 = \boxed{}$

Step Ahead   Anya had some money that was less than one dollar. She spent 36 cents of the amount.

a. How much might Anya have had at the start? $\boxed{}$ cents

b. Use your answer from above to complete this equation.

$\boxed{} - \boxed{} = \boxed{}$

Computation Practice

★ Complete these facts as fast as you can.

start 5 + 7 = ☐   15 − 6 = ☐   8 + 3 = ☐

7 − 3 = ☐   2 + 4 = ☐   12 − 5 = ☐

9 + 7 = ☐   17 − 8 = ☐   6 + 2 = ☐

8 − 3 = ☐   3 + 1 = ☐   9 − 5 = ☐

3 + 9 = ☐   16 − 7 = ☐   1 + 6 = ☐

13 − 8 = ☐   4 + 8 = ☐   11 − 5 = ☐

8 + 9 = ☐   14 − 6 = ☐   finish

ORIGO Stepping Stones · Grade 2 · 8.2

© ORIGO Education

Ongoing Practice

1. Write the difference. Then draw jumps on the number line to show your thinking.

a.

$57 - 13 = \boxed{}$

b.

$78 - 24 = \boxed{}$

2. Write the number of tens and ones. Then write the total.

a.

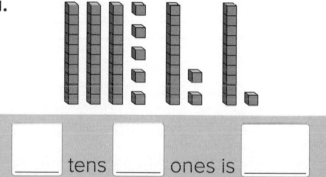

$\boxed{}$ tens $\boxed{}$ ones is $\boxed{}$

b.

$\boxed{}$ tens $\boxed{}$ ones is $\boxed{}$

Preparing for Module 9

Write the totals. You can use this piece of hundred chart to help.

a. $6 + 10 = \boxed{}$

b. $3 + 20 = \boxed{}$

c. $40 + 9 = \boxed{}$

d. $7 + 30 = \boxed{}$

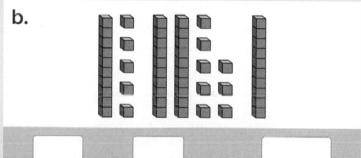

1	2	3	4	5	6	7	8	9	10
11	12	13	14	15	16	17	18	19	20
21	22	23	24	25	26	27	28	29	30
31	32	33	34	35	36	37	38	39	40
41	42	43	44	45	46	47	48	49	50

Step In

There are 62 pages in the book.
Anna reads 15 pages before bed.

How many pages are left to read?

Lulu uses blocks to figure out the answer.
She drew these pictures to help.

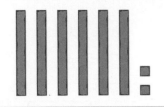

First she showed 62.

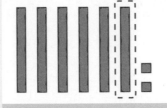

Then she regrouped
1 ten as 10 ones.

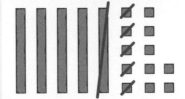

Then she crossed out 15 to
find the number left over.

Why do you think she regrouped 1 tens block for 10 ones blocks?

What is another way to figure out the answer?

Step Up

1. In the pictures below, a tens block has been regrouped as 10 ones blocks. Cross out blocks and complete the sentences to figure out the difference.

a.

$$34 - 8 = \boxed{}$$

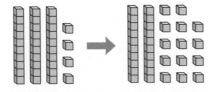

There are _____ tens.

There are _____ ones.

_____ and _____ is _____

b.

$$76 - 9 = \boxed{}$$

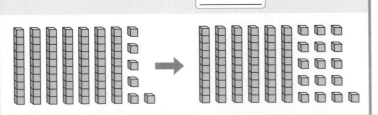

There are _____ tens.

There are _____ ones.

_____ and _____ is _____

2. In each picture, a tens block was regrouped as 10 ones blocks. Cross out blocks and complete the sentences to figure out the difference.

a.

65 − 27 = ☐

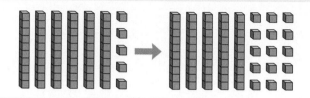

There are _____ tens.

There are _____ ones.

_____ and _____ is _____

b.

43 − 18 = ☐

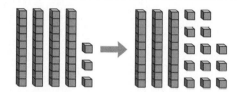

There are _____ tens.

There are _____ ones.

_____ and _____ is _____

c.

86 − 47 = ☐

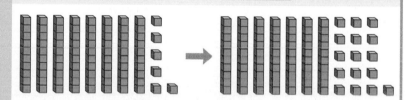

There are _____ tens.

There are _____ ones.

_____ and _____ is _____

3. Complete each equation. You can use blocks or make notes on page 318 to help.

a. 63 − 14 = ☐

b. 45 − 39 = ☐

c. 70 − 48 = ☐

Step Ahead Choose one equation from Question 3 that you could solve without using blocks. Show your method below.

Step In   Think about how you would solve each equation with blocks.

63 – 42 = ☐   47 – 19 = ☐   80 – 56 = ☐

Circle the equations that you would figure out using regrouping.
How did you decide which equations to circle?

> I compared the number of ones. If I had to take away more ones than were there, then I knew I had to regroup a ten.

How would you use blocks to figure out 47 – 19?

What steps would you follow?

Step Up   I.   Draw pictures to show how to regroup. Then complete the equation.

a.   81 – 45 = ☐

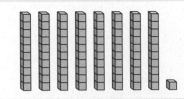

b.   57 – 39 = ☐

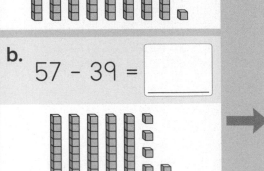

© ORIGO Education

2. Complete each equation. Show your thinking.

a.

$38 - 19 =$ ⬜

b.

$42 - 25 =$ ⬜

c.

$51 - 37 =$ ⬜

d.

$76 - 28 =$ ⬜

Step Ahead

There are 80 stickers in a pack. 25 stickers are handed out in the first week of school. 19 stickers are handed out in the second week. How many stickers are left in the pack? Show your thinking.

⬜ stickers

Think and Solve Lisa bought **four** items for a total of **$7**.

$1 each $3 each $2 each $4 each

a. Write the items that you think she bought.

b. Lisa used a $20 bill to pay for the items. How much money should she get back? $_____

Words at Work   Write a subtraction word problem in which you need to regroup a ten to figure out the answer. You can use words from the list to help you.

how many

figure out

difference

total

count

Ongoing Practice

1. Figure out the difference. Draw jumps on the number line to show your thinking. Then complete the equations.

FROM 2.7.4

a.

$46 – $25 = $ _____

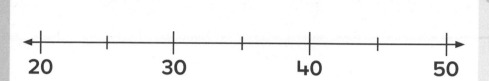
20   30   40   50

b.

$32 – $14 = $ _____

10   20   30   40

2. In this picture, a tens block was regrouped as 10 ones blocks. Cross out blocks and complete the sentences to figure out the difference.

FROM 2.8.3

74 – 36 = _____

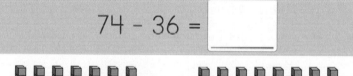

There are _____ tens.

There are _____ ones.

_____ and _____ is _____

Preparing for Module 9

Draw jumps to show how you could count on to figure out each of these. Then write the total.

a.

52 + 17 = _____

40   50   60   70

b.

63 + 25 = _____

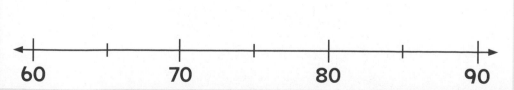
60   70   80   90

Step In Imagine you cut off 39 inches from this piece of wood.

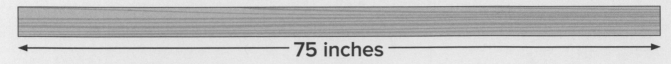

75 inches

What is an easy way to estimate the length of the piece left over?

39 is close to 40, so I think 75 – 40.

Imagine the full length is 45 inches and you cut off a piece that is 16 inches long. How would you estimate 45 – 16?

16 is close to 15, so I think 45 – 15 to make it easier.

Step Up 1. Estimate the **difference** between these lengths. Then write an equation to show your thinking.

a.

29 in   54 in

The difference is about [ ] in. _____

b.

96 in   36 in

The difference is about [ ] in. _____

c.

46 in   85 in

The difference is about [ ] in. _____

© ORIGO Education

2. Read each problem. Then color the label to show your **estimate**.

a. The movie runs for 96 minutes. Evan pauses the movie after 54 minutes to make some popcorn. About how many more minutes will the movie run?

| 30 minutes | 40 minutes | 50 minutes |

b. Brianna had $57. She spent $29 on flowers, and $11 on a book. About how much money does she have left?

| $10 | $20 | $30 |

c. Hernando is driving to the beach. The total distance is 85 miles. He has driven 14 miles. About how many more miles does he need to drive?

| 70 miles | 80 miles | 90 miles |

d. Carol plays basketball. She scores 18 points in her first season and 61 points in her second season. About how many more points did she score in her second season?

| 30 points | 40 points | 50 points |

3. Estimate each difference. Color the cards that have a difference of **about 50**.

| a. 51 – 30 | b. 78 – 65 | c. 63 – 15 | d. 94 – 39 | e. 82 – 17 |

| f. 45 – 21 | g. 72 – 24 | h. 64 – 55 | i. 82 – 34 | j. 98 – 31 |

Step Ahead Color two ribbons that have a difference of about 30 inches in length.

32 inches

12 inches

45 inches

74 inches

© ORIGO Education

Step In

Class 2B students have collected 124 cereal box tops. They have collected 19 more box tops than Class 2A.

How many box tops have Class 2A collected?

Is this problem about addition or subtraction?
How can you tell?

Do you think that the difference is more or less than 100? How do you know?

Corey follows these steps to figure out the difference.

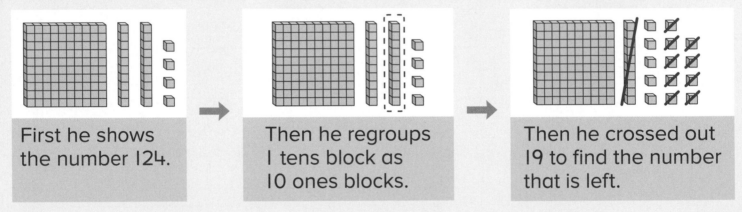

First he shows the number 124.

Then he regroups 1 tens block as 10 ones blocks.

Then he crossed out 19 to find the number that is left.

Why do you think he regrouped 1 tens blocks as 10 ones blocks?

How do the blocks show the solution to the problem?

Step Up

1. In each picture below, a tens block was regrouped as 10 ones blocks. Cross out blocks and complete the equations.

a. 121 – 15 = ☐

b. 135 – 28 = ☐

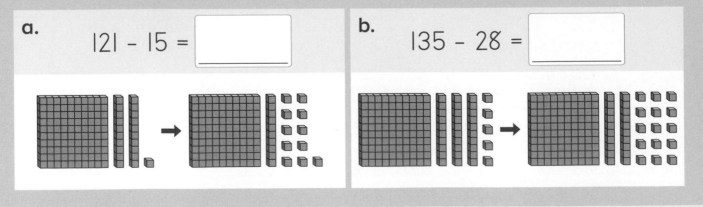

2. Complete each equation. Show your thinking.

a. 127 – 18 = [ ]

b. 131 – 26 = [ ]

c. 140 – 23 = [ ]

3. Complete each equation. You can use blocks or make notes on page 318 to help.

a. 124 – 15 = [ ]

b. 130 – 18 = [ ]

c. 108 – 24 = [ ]

d. 136 – 52 = [ ]

e. 122 – 17 = [ ]

f. 102 – 41 = [ ]

Step Ahead Write an equation to match each story. Each equation should use two-digit numbers and three-digit numbers. Each story has more than one possible answer.

a. Akari had to regroup a tens block to subtract 4 ones.

[ ] – [ ] = [ ]

b. Peter had to regroup a hundreds block to subtract 6 tens.

[ ] – [ ] = [ ]

Computation Practice

★ Write the totals in the grid below.

Across	Down
a. 34 + 33	**a.** 31 + 32
b. 21 + 23	**b.** 23 + 21
c. 11 + 12	**c.** 13 + 11
d. 43 + 41	**d.** 44 + 42
e. 32 + 34	**e.** 33 + 32
g. 43 + 42	**f.** 44 + 43
h. 13 + 14	**g.** 42 + 41
i. 21 + 22	**h.** 12 + 13
j. 23 + 22	

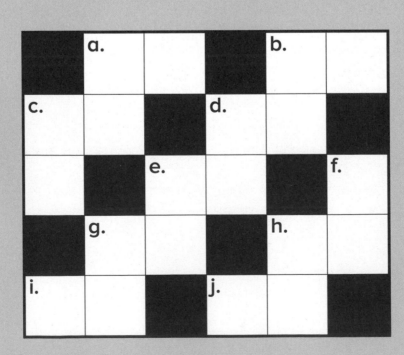

Ongoing Practice

1. Figure out the difference. Draw jumps to show your thinking.

a.

$56 - 28 = \boxed{}$

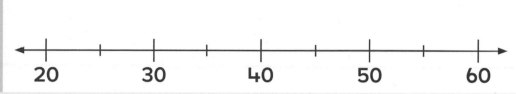

20   30   40   50   60

b.

$65 - 28 = \boxed{}$

30   40   50   60   70

2. Estimate the difference between these lengths. Then write an equation to show your thinking.

18 in		34 in

The difference is about $\boxed{}$ in. $\boxed{}$

Preparing for Module 9   Complete each equation. Show your thinking.

a.

$37 + 34 = \boxed{}$

b.

$28 + 56 = \boxed{}$

Step In Look at the scoreboard.

HOME 126   VISITORS 80

Do you think the home team won by greater or fewer than 50 points? How do you know?

How would you figure out the exact difference?

Marvin uses blocks. He follows these steps.

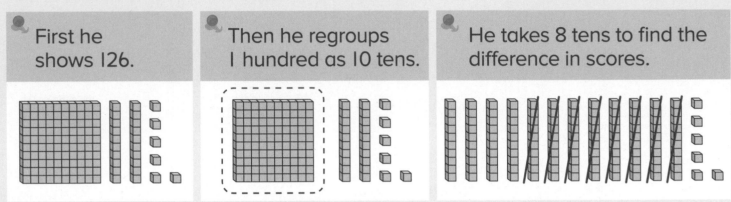

First he shows 126.

Then he regroups 1 hundred as 10 tens.

He takes 8 tens to find the difference in scores.

Why do you think he regrouped 1 hundreds block as 10 tens blocks?

How many points did the home team win by?

Step Up 1. In each picture, a hundreds block was regrouped as 10 tens blocks. Cross out blocks and complete the equations.

a.
$$110 - 30 = \boxed{}$$

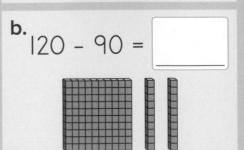

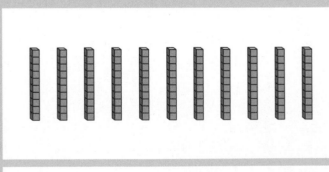

b.
$$120 - 90 = \boxed{}$$

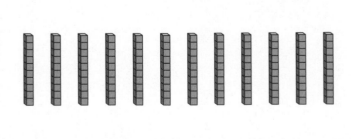

2. Draw pictures to show how to regroup. Then complete the equations.

a.
115 – 30 =

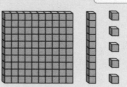 ➡

b.
124 – 60 = [ ]

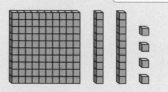 ➡

c.
128 – 50 = [ ]

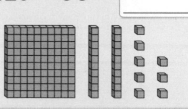 ➡

3. Complete each equation. You can use blocks or make notes on page 318 to help.

a. 110 – 90 = [ ]

b. 125 – 30 = [ ]

c. 108 – 20 = [ ]

Step Ahead Two teams are playing a game of basketball. The blue team scores 36 more points than the red team. The blue team scores 110 points. How many points does the red team score? Show your thinking.

[ ] points

Step In

A farmer collects 126 eggs on Monday and 54 eggs on Wednesday.

Do you think the difference is greater or fewer than 50? How did you decide?

Brady uses blocks to figure out the difference.

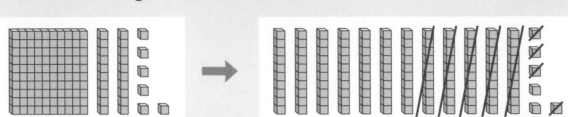

What steps does he follow?

How many more eggs were collected on Monday than Wednesday?

What equation would you write?

There are 7 tens and 2 ones left over.

$$126 - 54 = 72$$

Step Up

1. Write the number of tens and ones that are left. Cross out blocks to help. Then write the difference.

a.
$$127 - 35 = \boxed{}$$

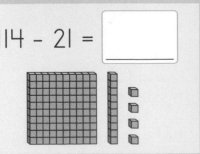

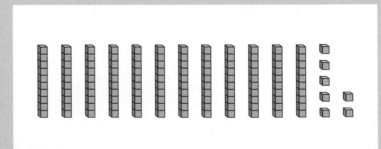

b.
$$114 - 21 = \boxed{}$$

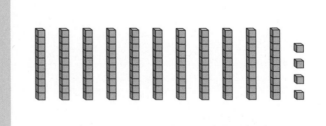

2. Draw pictures to show how to regroup. Then complete the equations.

a.
114 − 62 = [ ]

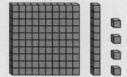

➡️

b.
135 − 54 = [ ]

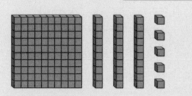

➡️

c.
107 − 36 = [ ]

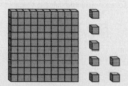

➡️

3. Complete each equation. You can use blocks or make notes on page 318 to help.

a.
124 − 82 = [ ]

b.
116 − 85 = [ ]

c.
105 − 34 = [ ]

Step Ahead

Read the number of hundreds, tens, and ones. Then write the same value with tens and ones only.

a. 1 hundred 2 tens 5 ones shows the same number as

[ ] tens and [ ] ones

b. 1 hundred 0 tens 2 ones shows the same number as

[ ] tens and [ ] ones

Think and Solve

The picture on the left below is a magic X. The total of the numbers in each straight line is the same. The magic total is 9.

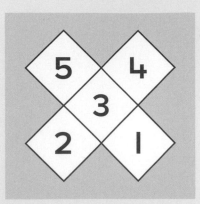

Use these numbers to make a magic X with a magic total of 15.

1	3	5
	7	9

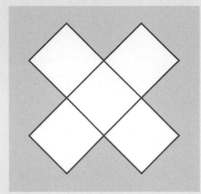

Words at Work   Write in words how you solve this problem.

Charlotte buys some flowers for $15 and a book for $26. She has $14 left. How much money did she have before she went shopping?

Ongoing Practice

1. Write the number of sides inside each polygon. Write **N** inside the shapes that are **not** polygons.

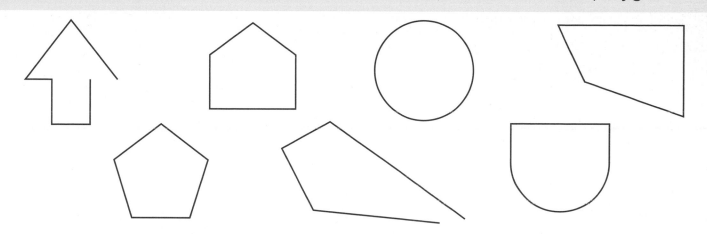

2. Draw pictures to show how to regroup. Then complete the equations.

a.
126 – 43 = ☐

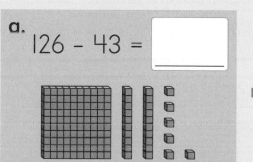

b.
105 – 31 = ☐

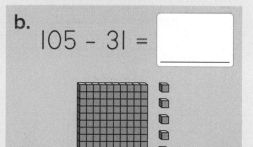

Preparing for Module 9

Complete each equation.

a. 70 + 70 = ☐

b. 60 + 48 = ☐

c. 36 + 80 = ☐

d. 30 + 94 = ☐

e. 50 + 75 = ☐

f. 97 + 40 = ☐

Step In

Count in steps of five around this clock.

Write the numbers you say.

What happens when you reach 12 on the clock?

How many minutes past the hour is a half-past time? How do you know?

How many minutes past the hour is this clock showing?

Which hour is it?

What time is the clock showing?

What is another way you could read this time?

What time is showing on this clock?

How do you know?

Step Up

I. Write each time.

a.

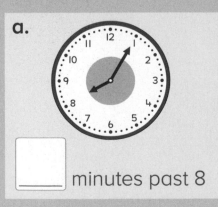

_____ minutes past 8

b.

_____ minutes past 9

c.

_____ minutes past 4

2. Write numbers to show each time.

a.

_____ minutes past _____

b.

_____ minutes past _____

c.

_____ minutes past _____

d.

_____ minutes past _____

e.

_____ minutes past _____

f.

_____ minutes past _____

Step Ahead

Count in steps of five to figure out how many minutes have passed.

a.

start   finish

_____ minutes

b.

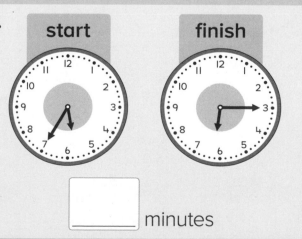

start   finish

_____ minutes

Step In What time is showing on this digital clock?

How would you show the same time on an analog clock?
How do you know?

Look at this clock.
Why is there a zero just before the five?

How would you show the same time
on an analog clock? How do you know?

**What different ways could you say
the time shown on this clock?**

Twenty past nine.

Nine twenty.

Step Up

I. Draw lines to connect the matching times.
Cross out the digital clock that does not have a match.

 2:35

3:45

 7:20

10:15

 7:10

2. Draw lines to connect clocks to times.
Cross out the two clocks that do **not** have a match.

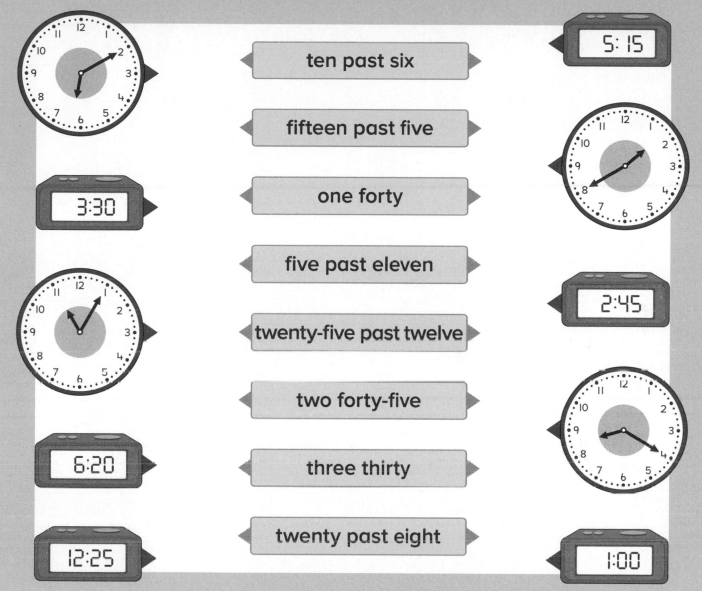

ten past six

fifteen past five

one forty

five past eleven

twenty-five past twelve

two forty-five

three thirty

twenty past eight

5:15

3:30

2:45

6:20

12:25

1:00

Step Ahead

In each pattern, the next clock shows **five minutes more**.
Complete the missing times.

a.

b.   [:]   [:]   3:05   3:10   3:15

Computation Practice

What did the ocean say to the people on the beach?

★ Complete the equations.
★ Then write each letter above its matching total at the bottom of the page.

Some letters are used more than once.

26 + 33 = ☐ **a**

45 + 48 = ☐ **o**

67 + 24 = ☐ **t**

82 + 16 = ☐ **w**

24 + 18 = ☐ **i**

38 + 38 = ☐ **d**

72 + 27 = ☐ **j**

39 + 14 = ☐ **h**

47 + 31 = ☐ **s**

15 + 29 = ☐ **n**

28 + 67 = ☐ **g**

36 + 61 = ☐ **e**

26 + 45 = ☐ **u**

56 + 32 = ☐ **v**

☐ ☐ ☐ ☐ ☐ ☐ ☐ ,
44 93 91 53 42 44 95

☐ ☐   ☐ ☐ ☐ ☐   ☐ ☐ ☐ ☐ ☐
42 91   99 71 78 91   98 59 88 97 76

1. Use your ruler to draw more straight sides to make three quadrilaterals.

a. 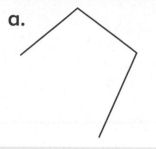 b. 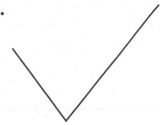 c.

FROM 2.7.10

2. Write numbers to show each time.

a.

_____ minutes past _____

b.

_____ minutes past _____

FROM 2.8.9

c.

_____ minutes past _____

d.

_____ minutes past _____

Preparing for Module 9

a. Draw a pencil that is 4 inches long.
b. Draw a pencil that is shorter than 4 inches.

```
0 inches   1    2    3    4    5    6
```

Step In   Look at this analog clock.

Where will the hands be pointing when the time is 11 o'clock? How do you know?

Where will the hands be pointing when the time is half past 11? How do you know?

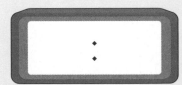

How many minutes has the minute hand moved past the hour on this clock?

What are the different ways you could read or say the time shown on the clock?

Fifteen minutes past nine,   nine fifteen, and   quarter past nine.

How could you show the same time on this digital clock?

How do you know?

Step Up   1.   Write the matching time on the digital clock.

a.

b.

c.
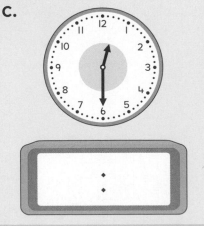

2. Draw hands on the analog clock to show the matching time.

a.

b.

c.

3. Write each time two different ways.

a.

quarter past ____

____ minutes past ____

b.

half past ____

____ minutes past ____

c.
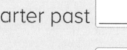
quarter past ____

____ minutes past ____

d.
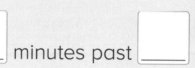
half past ____

____ minutes past ____

Step Ahead Complete the clocks to keep each pattern going.

a.

b.

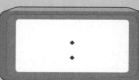
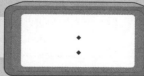

10:30 11:30 12:30

© ORIGO Education

Step In

At what time does a day begin?
What time does it end? How do you know?

What time is exactly in the middle of the day?

Look at the clock. What do you know about this time of the day?

How could you show the difference between 6 o'clock in the morning and 6 o'clock in the evening?

We write **a.m.** to describe times **between midnight and noon**.

We write **p.m.** to describe times **between noon and midnight**.

a.m. is short for **ante meridiem** which means **before noon**.
p.m. is short for **post meridiem** which means **after noon**.

Step Up

1. Write the digital time for each event.
Then write **a.m.** or **p.m.** to match the event.

a.   eat breakfast

b.   walk home from school

c.   prepare for dinner

d.   pack lunch

2. Write each of these as digital times. Circle **a.m.** or **p.m.**

a. twenty-five minutes past ten in the morning

☐ : ☐   a.m.   p.m.

b. seven forty-five at night

☐ : ☐   a.m.   p.m.

c. fifteen minutes past three in the afternoon

☐ : ☐   a.m.   p.m.

d. ten minutes past eleven at night

☐ : ☐   a.m.   p.m.

e. quarter past eleven in the morning

☐ : ☐   a.m.   p.m.

f. four fifty in the afternoon

☐ : ☐   a.m.   p.m.

g. ten thirty at night

☐ : ☐   a.m.   p.m.

h. eight fifteen at night

☐ : ☐   a.m.   p.m.

Step Ahead   Kyle and Emma live in different towns. Their families are driving to the same campsite for a vacation.

Kyle's family will leave at 9 p.m. on Friday. Their journey will take 10 hours. Emma's family will leave at 3 a.m. on Saturday. Their journey will take 5 hours.

a. Whose family will reach the campsite first?

_____

b. At what time of day will they arrive?

_____

© ORIGO Education

Think and Solve

You can only move ⟶ or ↑.

•——• is 1 unit.

How many units are in the **shortest** path from Home to School?

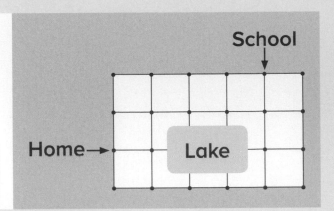

School

Home→ Lake

Words at Work

Imagine your friend was away from school when you learned about using a.m. and p.m. Write how you would explain the terms to your friend.

1. Draw a shape to match each label.

a.	a triangle with no sides the same length	b.	a quadrilateral with exactly two sides the same length

FROM 2.7.12

2. Write the digital time for each event. Then write **a.m.** or **p.m.** to match the event.

a. wake up

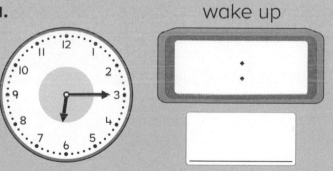

b. eat lunch

FROM 2.8.12

Find and record two objects at home to match each length.

a. Between 1 yard and 2 yards long	b. Between 2 yards and 3 yards long

Step In

There were 105 students in the playground. 3 more students joined them. How many students are there now?

It's such a small jump, so it's easy to do in my head. I'll use what I know from my basic addition facts.

Sara showed her thinking on this number line.

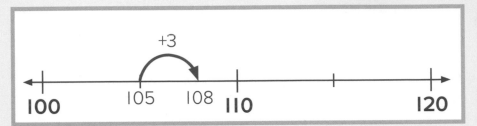

What other addition problems greater than 100 do you think you could solve easily?

Step Up

1. Count on and write the totals. Show your thinking.

a.

126 + 2 = ☐

<-----|----------|----------|----------|----------|----->
     120   130   140

b.

116 + 3 = ☐

<-----|----------|----------|----------|----------|----->
     100   110   120

2. Figure out the totals. Then write the turnarounds.

a.
106 + 3 = ☐

☐ + ☐ = ☐

b.
146 + 1 = ☐

☐ + ☐ = ☐

3. Complete each equation. Show your thinking.

a.

153 + 10 = ⬚

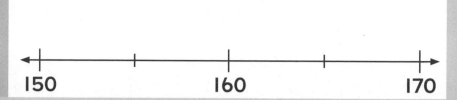

150   160   170

b.

238 + 20 = ⬚

230   240   250   260

c.

142 + 30 = ⬚

4. Figure out the totals. Then write the turnarounds.

a.

234 + 30 = ⬚

⬚ + ⬚ = ⬚

b.

275 + 20 = ⬚

⬚ + ⬚ = ⬚

5. Think of the turnarounds to help you figure out the totals.

a.
10 + 238 = ⬚

b.
1 + 156 = ⬚

c.
3 + 266 = ⬚

Step Ahead   Write the missing numbers along this trail.

321 → +2 → ⬚ → +30 → ⬚ → +3 → ⬚ → +20 → ⬚

Step In **A school play is being held in the gym.**

Last week, 453 tickets were sold. An extra 32 tickets were sold yesterday. How could you figure out the total number of tickets that have been sold?

José showed his thinking on a number line.

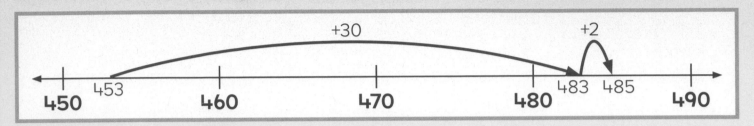

What other jumps could be made to figure out the total?

Abigail used blocks to help figure out the total.

How many hundreds are there in total? How many tens? How many ones?

Step Up **I.** Complete each equation. Show your thinking.

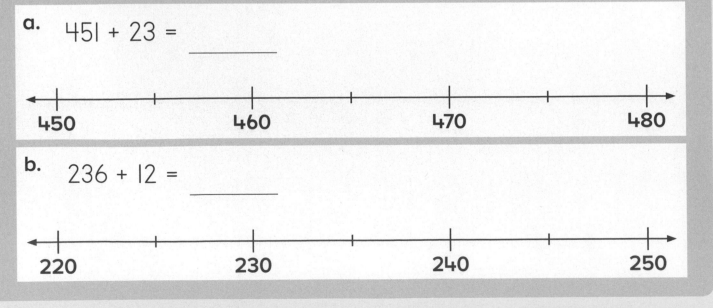

a. 451 + 23 = _____

b. 236 + 12 = _____

2. Complete each equation. Show your thinking.

a.

374 + 13 = _____

b.

528 + 31 = _____

3. Write the number of hundreds, tens, and ones. Then write
an equation to show the total. You can use blocks to help.

a.   **625 + 14**

There are [ ] hundreds.

There are [ ] tens.

There are [ ] ones.

_____ + _____ + _____ = _____

b.   **352 + 26**

There are [ ] hundreds.

There are [ ] tens.

There are [ ] ones.

_____ + _____ + _____ = _____

Step Ahead   Write the missing digits to make each equation true.

a. [ ] 7 [ ] + [ ] 5 [ ] = 2 8 7

b. 1 [ ] 4 + 3 [ ] = 1 7 6

c. [ ] 2 [ ] + [ ] 6 [ ] = 8 5 7

Computation Practice

Why were two spiders playing soccer on a saucer?

★ Complete these equations.
★ Then write each letter above its matching answer at the bottom of the page.

12 − 8 = ☐ **r**	11 − 5 = ☐ **t**	7 + 8 = ☐ **a**
5 + 9 = ☐ **w**	16 − 7 = ☐ **o**	14 − 6 = ☐ **h**
9 + 4 = ☐ **c**	8 + 9 = ☐ **i**	12 − 9 = ☐ **g**
5 − 3 = ☐ **y**	3 + 8 = ☐ **u**	7 + 5 = ☐ **n**
13 − 8 = ☐ **f**	2 + 8 = ☐ **c**	9 + 7 = ☐ **e**
4 + 3 = ☐ **p**		

Some letters appear more than once.

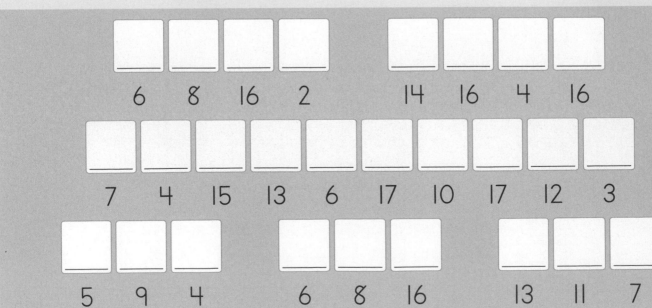

☐ ☐ ☐ ☐   ☐ ☐ ☐ ☐
6 8 16 2   14 16 4 16

☐ ☐ ☐ ☐ ☐ ☐ ☐ ☐ ☐
7 4 15 13 6 17 10 17 12 3

☐ ☐ ☐   ☐ ☐ ☐   ☐ ☐ ☐
5 9 4   6 8 16   13 11 7

Ongoing Practice

1. Write the number of tens and ones.
   Then write the total.

a.
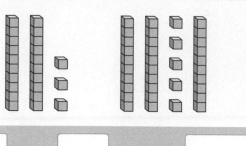

☐ tens ☐ ones is ☐

b.
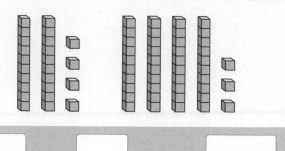

☐ tens ☐ ones is ☐

2. Think of the turnarounds to help figure out the totals.

a.
356 + 10 = ☐

b.
368 + 20 = ☐

c.
355 + 30 = ☐

d.
10 + 374 = ☐

e.
20 + 361 = ☐

f.
30 + 359 = ☐

Preparing for Module 10

Draw pictures to show how to regroup.
Then complete the equations.

a.
117 – 80 = ☐

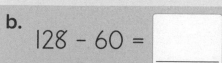

→

b.
128 – 60 = ☐

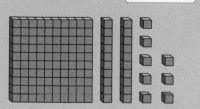

→

Step In How could you figure out the total cost of the guitar and speaker?

Mia used blocks to help figure out the total cost.

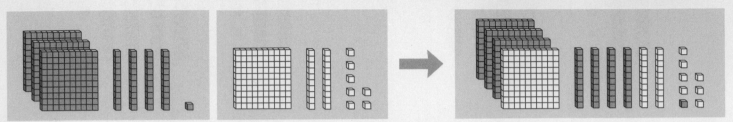

How many hundreds are there in total? How many tens? How many ones?

Terek used a number line to figure it out.

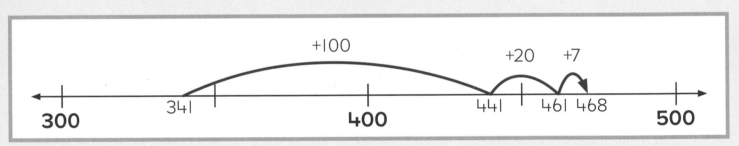

What number did he start with? How did he break up the other number?

Step Up

1. Write the number of hundreds, tens, and ones. Then write an equation to show the total. You can use blocks to help.

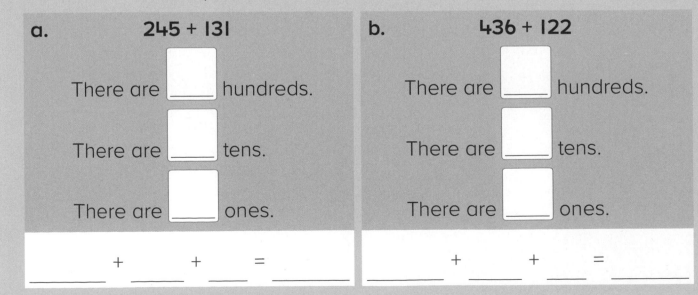

a. 245 + 131

There are ____ hundreds.

There are ____ tens.

There are ____ ones.

____ + ____ + ____ = ____

b. 436 + 122

There are ____ hundreds.

There are ____ tens.

There are ____ ones.

____ + ____ + ____ = ____

2. Complete each equation. Show your thinking.

a. 257 + 112 = _____

|———+————————+———————+————+——▶
200   300   400

b. 748 + 131 = _____

|———+————————+———————+————+——▶
700   800   900

c. 231 + 124 = _____

◀————————————————————————————————▶

3. Use a thinking strategy to solve each of these. You can record your thinking on page 356.

a. 372 + 113 = [_____]

b. 153 + 124 = [_____]

c. 520 + 124 = [_____]

Step Ahead   Each brick shows the total of the two numbers directly below. Write the missing numbers.

a.

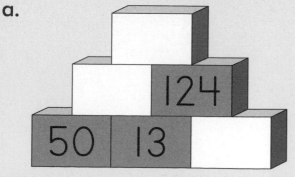

b.

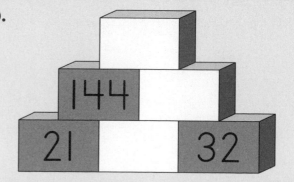

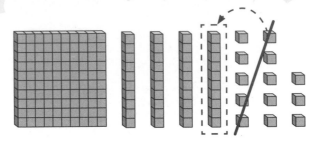

Step In **Look at this picture of blocks.**

What number does it show?
How do you know?

What could you do with the ones blocks to make 4 tens blocks
and keep the total the same?

I could regroup 10 ones blocks as
1 tens block. That makes 4 tens blocks
and the total does not change.

Look at this picture.

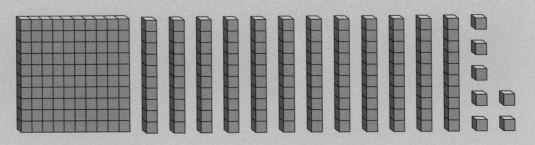

What could you do with the blocks to make 2 hundreds blocks
and keep the total the same?

How many tens blocks would you have?
How many ones blocks would there be?

Does the total change?

© ORIGO Education

Read the number of hundreds, tens, and ones. Write the number to match. Show your thinking.

a. 2 hundreds, 1 ten, and 13 ones

(is the same value as)

b. 3 hundreds, 8 tens, and 18 ones

(is the same value as)

c. 1 hundreds, 2 tens, and 16 ones

(is the same value as)

d. 7 hundreds, 3 tens, and 36 ones

(is the same value as)

e. 7 hundreds, 16 tens, and 2 ones

(is the same value as)

f. 2 hundreds, 14 tens, and 6 ones

(is the same value as)

Step Ahead

Look at this picture of blocks.

Figure out and write the number that it shows.

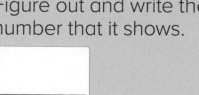

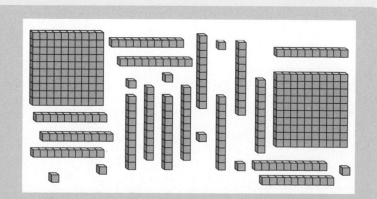

Think and Solve Imagine you threw three beanbags and they all hit this target.

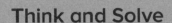

a. Write the greatest and least possible totals.

greatest | least
| | |

b. Write an equation to show one way you can make a **total of 80**.

☐ + ☐ + ☐ = 80

c. Write equations to show **two other ways** you can make a total of 80.

☐ + ☐ + ☐ = 80   ☐ + ☐ + ☐ = 80

Words at Work   Write about some different ways you can split 365 into hundreds, tens and ones. You can use words from the list to help.

hundreds
tens
ones
regroup
parts

© ORIGO Education

I. Look at each picture of blocks. Write the matching number with and without the expander.

a.

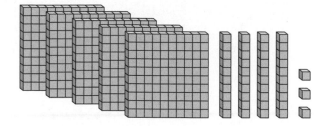

hundreds

b.

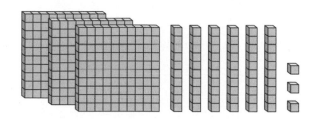

hundreds

2. Draw jumps to show how you could figure out the total. Then write the total.

$634 + 152 =$ _____

Draw pictures to show how to regroup. Then complete the equations.

a. $138 - 62 =$ ☐

b. $159 - 73 =$ ☐

FROM 2.1.8

FROM 2.9.3

Step In Look at these pictures of blocks.

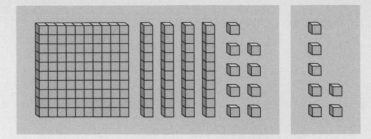

What numbers do they show?
What is the total?
What would you do with the 16 ones?

What is another way you could figure out the total?

I could use a number line like this.

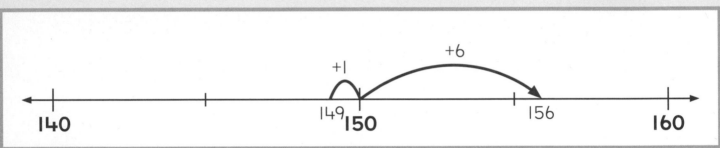

How would you add the numbers in your head?

Step Up 1. Write the number of hundreds, tens, and ones. Then write an equation to show the total. You can use blocks to help.

a. **345 + 7**

There are ____ hundreds.

There are ____ tens.

There are ____ ones.

____ + ____ + ____ = ____

b. **287 + 8**

There are ____ hundreds.

There are ____ tens.

There are ____ ones.

____ + ____ + ____ = ____

2. Draw jumps to show how you add to find each total.
Then write the total.

a.
$139 + 5 =$ ⬜

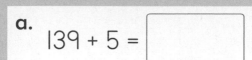

130		140	150

b.
$168 + 3 =$ ⬜

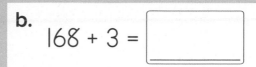

160		170	180

c.
$576 + 8 =$ ⬜

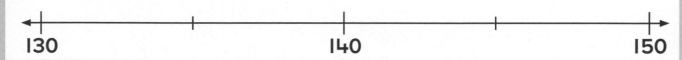

d.
$807 + 6 =$ ⬜

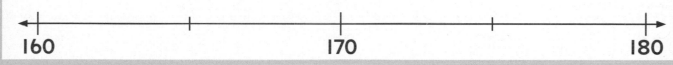

Step Ahead   Write an equation to match the story. Then write the total.

On Monday, Donna walked 538 steps from her front door to the bus stop.
On Tuesday, she counted her steps again. She found that she had walked
6 more steps than on Monday. How many steps did she take on Tuesday?

⬜

Step In Look at these pictures of blocks.

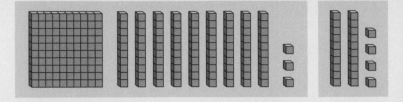

What numbers do they show?

How could you figure out the total?

Isaac added on a number line like this.

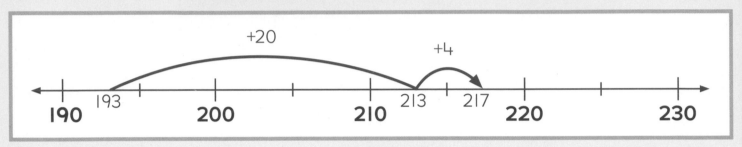

Draw jumps on this number line to show another way to find the total.

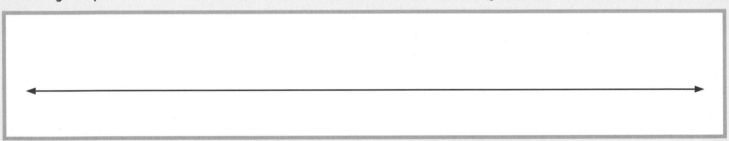

Step Up

I. Write the number of hundreds, tens, and ones. Then write an equation to show the total. You can use blocks to help.

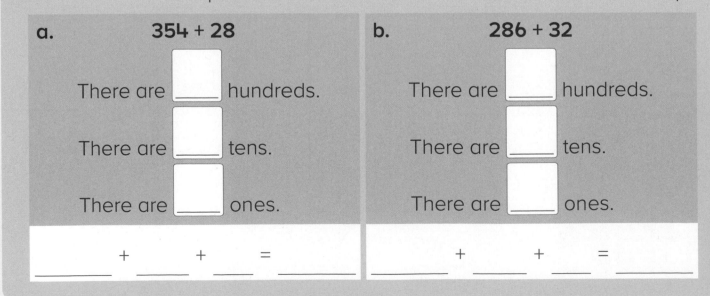

a. **354 + 28**

There are ____ hundreds.

There are ____ tens.

There are ____ ones.

____ + ____ + ____ = ____

b. **286 + 32**

There are ____ hundreds.

There are ____ tens.

There are ____ ones.

____ + ____ + ____ = ____

© ORIGO Education

2. Draw jumps to show how you could figure out each total.
Then write the total.

a.

328 + 25 = [ ]

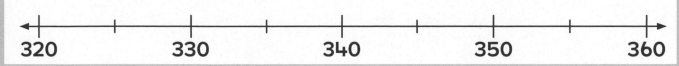

320   330   340   350   360

b.

637 + 27 = [ ]

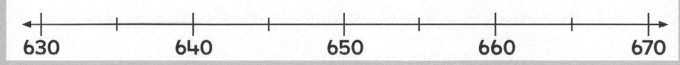

630   640   650   660   670

c.

797 + 26 = [ ]

d.

488 + 32 = [ ]

Step Ahead Jack bought a game console and one game. He had $200 and got some change. Circle the items he may have bought. There is more than one possible answer.

 $148
 $173
 BATTLESHIPS $57
 Grow A Garden $38
 $26

Computation Practice

Which foot did Neil Armstrong first put down on the moon?

★ Complete the equations. Then color the letters that show each total in the puzzle below.

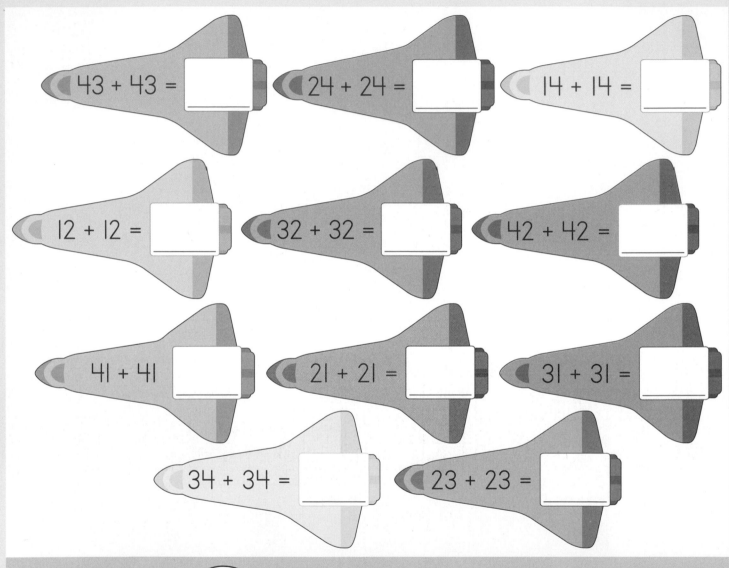

43 + 43 = [ ]

24 + 24 = [ ]

14 + 14 = [ ]

12 + 12 = [ ]

32 + 32 = [ ]

42 + 42 = [ ]

41 + 41 [ ]

21 + 21 = [ ]

31 + 31 = [ ]

34 + 34 = [ ]

23 + 23 = [ ]

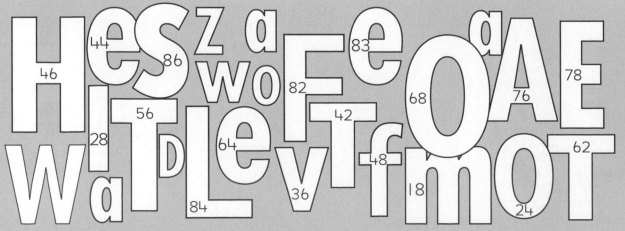

ORIGO Stepping Stones · Grade 2 · 9.6

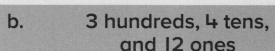
Ongoing Practice	**1.** Draw pictures to show how to regroup. Then complete the equation.

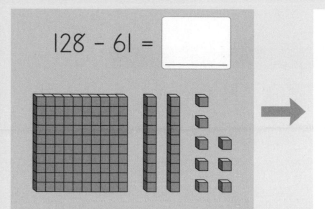

$128 - 61 =$ [ ]

2. Write the number of hundreds, tens, and ones. Then write an equation to show the total. You can use blocks to help.

a. **265 + 8**

There are [ ] hundreds.

There are [ ] tens.

There are [ ] ones.

___ + ___ + ___ = ___

b. **326 + 7**

There are [ ] hundreds.

There are [ ] tens.

There are [ ] ones.

___ + ___ + ___ = ___

Preparing for Module 10	Read the number of hundreds, tens, and ones. Write the matching numeral. Show your thinking.

a. 4 hundreds, 12 tens, and 5 ones

(is the same value as)

[ ]

b. 3 hundreds, 4 tens, and 12 ones

(is the same value as)

[ ]

Step In   Look at these two pieces of ribbon.

How could you figure out the total length?

345 in

173 in

Wendell added the parts of each number to find the total.
Write an equation to show his adding.

Draw jumps to show how you could add the numbers using a number line.

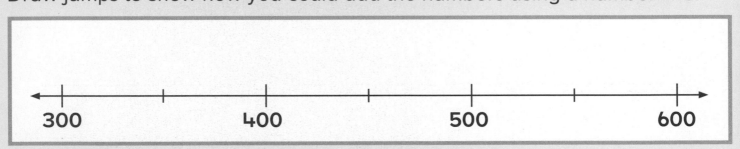

300   400   500   600

Which method do you like best? Why?

Step Up   **I.**   Write the number of hundreds, tens, and ones. Then write
an equation to show the total. You can use blocks to help.

a.   **252 + 129**   b.   **134 + 685**

There are ___ hundreds.   There are ___ hundreds.

There are ___ tens.   There are ___ tens.

There are ___ ones.   There are ___ ones.

___ + ___ + ___ = ___   ___ + ___ + ___ = ___

© ORIGO Education

2. Draw jumps to show how you could figure out each total.
Then write the totals.

a.

$458 + 138 =$ ☐

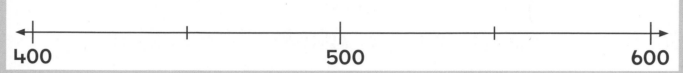

400   500   600

b.

$266 + 125 =$ ☐

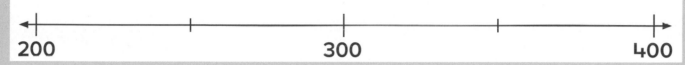

200   300   400

c.

$187 + 132 =$ ☐

d.

$381 + 136 =$ ☐

Step Ahead   Some students are joining cubes to make cube trains.

Carrina's cube train is 135 cubes long.

Isabelle's cube train is 116 cubes long.

Richard's cube train is 182 cubes long.

a. What is the longest cube train that can be made by joining two of their cube trains?

 cubes

b. What is the longest cube train they can make by joining all of their cube trains?

 cubes

Step In

Logan's family is buying some things to take on vacation. What do you think they will be doing?

How could you figure out the total cost of the tent and the chair?

What equations could you write to show your thinking?

 fishing rod $184

 umbrella $18

camp chair $23

 tent $435

Giselle added the places like this:

400 + 0 = 400
30 + 20 = 50
5 + 3 = 8
400 + 50 + 8 = 458

Katherine counted on the places like this:

435 + 20 = 455
455 + 3 = 458

Which method would you use to add numbers like this? Why?

Step Up

1. Figure out the total cost of each pair of items. You can use blocks or draw number lines on page 356 to help. Then write equations to show your thinking.

a. fishing rod and umbrella
Total $_____

b. tent and fishing rod
Total $_____

2. Figure out the total. You can use blocks or draw number lines on page 356 to help. Then write equations to show your thinking.

a.

146 + 38 = ___

b.

841 + 137 = ___

c.

135 + 617 = ___

d.

302 + 118 = ___

Step Ahead   Use each total as one of the parts of the next equation You can record your thinking on page 356.

188 + 31 = ___   →   ___ + 27 = ___

138 + ___ = ___   116 + ___ = ___

Think and Solve

a. Use different colors to show pairs of numbers that add to 100.

15	5	45	25	65
95	55	35	85	

b. Circle the number that is left over.

c. Use that number and complete this equation. ☐ + ☐ = 100

d. Use two numbers that are **not** shown above to complete this equation. ☐ + ☐ = 100

Words at Work

a. Write two different three-digit numbers that are less than 500. ☐ ☐

b. To find the total, you can add the parts of each number or start at the greater number and add the parts of the smaller number. Which strategy would you use to find the total? How did you decide?

Ongoing Practice

1. Complete the sentences and the equation.
You can cross out blocks to help.

a.

$79 - 14 = \boxed{}$

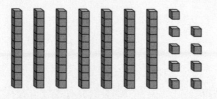

There are _____ tens.

There are _____ ones.

_____ and _____ is _____

b.

$67 - 22 = \boxed{}$

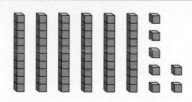

There are _____ tens.

There are _____ ones.

_____ and _____ is _____

2. Write the number of hundreds, tens, and ones. Then write an equation to show the total. You can use blocks to help.

a. 351 + 239 $\boxed{}$

There are _____ hundreds.

There are _____ tens.

There are _____ ones.

_____ + _____ + _____ = _____

b. 253 + 475 $\boxed{}$

There are _____ hundreds.

There are _____ tens.

There are _____ ones.

_____ + _____ + _____ = _____

Preparing for Module 10   Complete the equation. Show your thinking.

$72 - 38 = \boxed{}$

Step In   What are some things you know about a centimeter?

Each edge of a ones block is one centimeter long.

My finger is about one centimeter thick.

A ones block is one centimeter long. How long is a tens block?
How do you know?

Step Up

I. Use ones blocks and tens blocks to measure each of these lengths.

a. handspan ☐ centimeters long

b. palm ☐ centimeters long

c. index finger ☐ centimeters long

d. little finger ☐ centimeters long

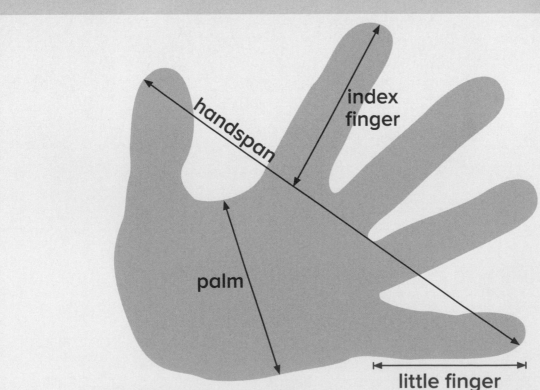

2. Trace around your hand like the hand in Question I.

3. Use ones blocks and tens blocks to measure each of these lengths.

a. handspan ____ centimeters long   b. palm ____ centimeters long

c. index finger ____ centimeters long   d. little finger ____ centimeters long

Step Ahead   Marcos stretched out some pieces of string he found.

The red string is 46 centimeters long.
The blue string is 48 centimeters long.
The green string is the same length
as the other two strings put together.
How long is the green string?

____ centimeters

Step In

What are some objects in the classroom that are about one centimeter long, one centimeter wide, or one centimeter thick?

What objects in the classroom are about 20 centimeters long? What is a quick way of measuring the length of these items?

What number should you start on when you measure with a ruler?

A short way to write centimeter is cm.

Step Up

1. a. Color green the object that you **think** is **about 5 cm long**.

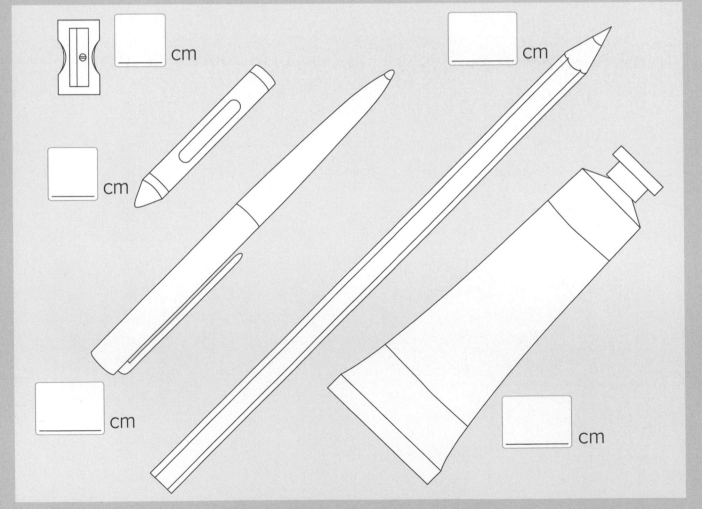

b. Use a ruler to measure the length of each object. Write the length in centimeters.

2. Use a ruler to measure the distance along each white strip. Mark the length and color the strip to match. The first one has been done for you.

  a. Measure 10 cm.

  b. Measure 6 cm.

  c. Measure 12 cm.

  d. Measure 15 cm.

  e. Measure 4 cm.

3. Look at the strip in Question 2d above. Use an inch ruler to measure the same part of the strip that you marked.

  a. **About** how long is that part of the strip? _____ inches

  b. Why are there fewer inches than centimeters?

Step Ahead

Samuel has two pet snakes. One snake is 36 cm long. The other snake is 87 cm long. Figure out the **difference** in length between the two snakes. Draw a number line to show your thinking.

_____ cm

Computation Practice

If you have six lemons in one hand and seven oranges in the other, what do you have?

★ Use a ruler to draw a straight line to each correct difference. The line will pass through a letter. Write each letter below its matching difference. The first one has been done for you.

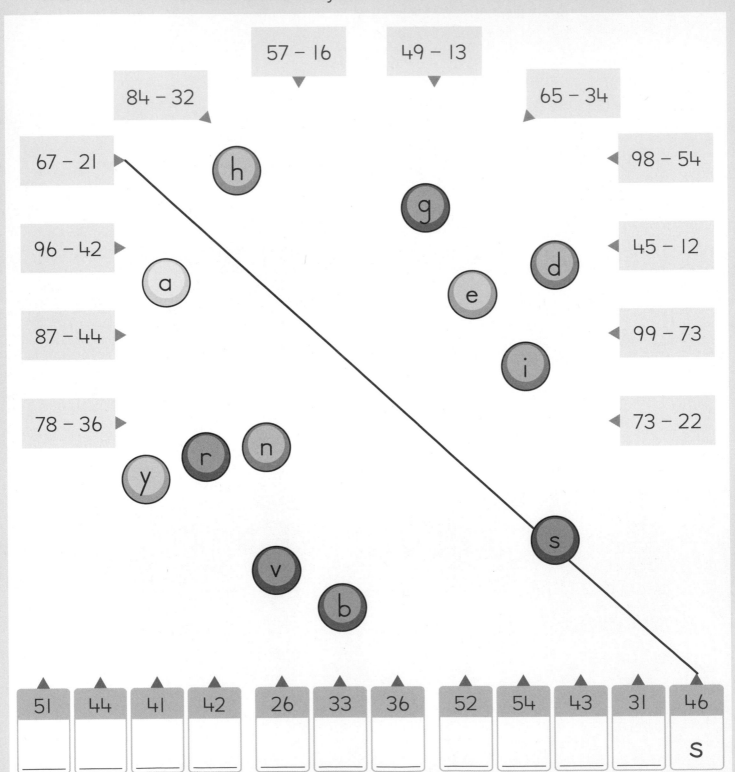

51	44	41	42	26	33	36	52	54	43	31	46
__	__	__	__	__	__	__	__	__	__	__	s

ORIGO Stepping Stones • Grade 2 • 9.10

Ongoing Practice

I. Write each time.

a.

_____ minutes past _____

b.

_____ minutes past _____

c.

_____ minutes past _____

d.

_____ minutes past _____

e.

_____ minutes past _____

f.

_____ minutes past _____

FROM 2.8.9

2. Measure the distance along each white strip. Mark the length and color the strip to match. The first one has been done for you.

a. Measure 11 cm.

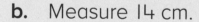

b. Measure 14 cm.

c. Measure 8 cm.

FROM 2.9.10

Preparing for Module 10 Complete the equation. Show your thinking.

152 – 47 = ◻

Step In   What do you know about meters?

Running races in the Olympic Games use meters. I know there is a 100-meter race and a 400-meter race.

A short way to write meter is m.

Four students threw small beanbags as part of a game.

These flags show where their beanbags landed.

Hailey   Andre   Leila   Luke

The distance between Hailey's throw and Andre's throw is one meter.

What do you think the distance is between Luke's throw and Leila's throw?

Why do you think that?

What other distances do you think you could figure out?

Step Up   I.   Four students threw beanbags. For each, write the distance of their beanbag throw or color the bar graph to show the result.

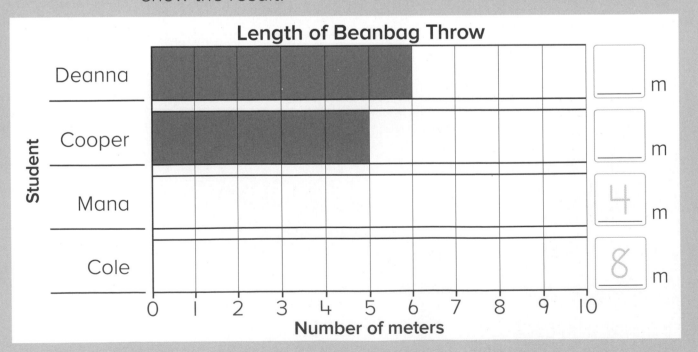

2. Use the graph on page 350 to complete these.

a. Cole threw ☐ meters farther than Cooper.

b. Mana's throw was ☐ meters shorter than Deanna's throw.

c. _____'s throw was half the distance of Cole's throw.

d. _____'s throw was one meter shorter than Cooper's.

e. _____'s throw was shorter than Cole's and farther than Cooper's.

f. Write the names in order from the shortest to the longest throw.

3. a. Imagine the throws were measured in feet. Would Mana's throw be longer or shorter than 4 feet?

b. Imagine the throws were measured in yards. Would Mana's throw be longer or shorter than 4 yards?

Step Ahead   Look at the table. Figure out these total lengths.

a. Gray whale and orca ☐ m

b. Bowhead whale and right whale ☐ m

c. Minke whale and blue whale ☐ m

Type of Whale	Length
Right whale	18 m
Gray whale	14 m
Minke whale	9 m
Orca	8 m
Bowhead whale	18 m
Blue whale	34 m

Step In

Ten students measured the distance from their wrist to their elbow.

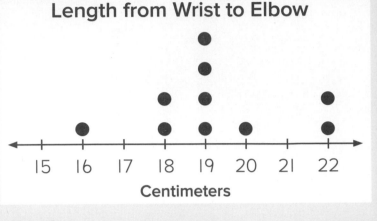

They showed their measurements in the graph on the right.

What do you think the numbers and dots mean?

This type of graph is called a **line plot** or **dot plot**.
The numbers show the lengths.
Each dot represents one student.

ℹ Keeping each row of dots in a straight line makes it easier to read.

How many students had a measurement of 19 cm?

What was the longest measurement recorded?
How many students had that measurement?

Step Up

1. Gemma measured the length of some pencils in her pencil case. She recorded the results in this table. Use the measurements to complete the line plot below.

14 cm	13 cm	9 cm	18 cm	13 cm	10 cm	17 cm
12 cm	18 cm	17 cm	15 cm	11 cm	17 cm	10 cm

Cross out each number in the table above after you record it in the line plot.

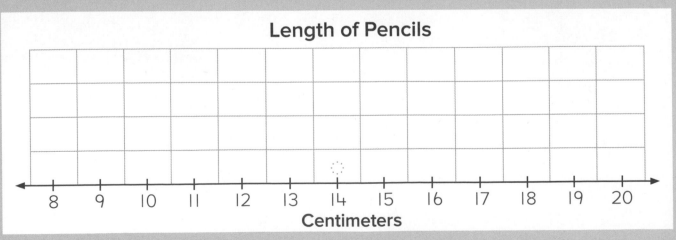

Length of Pencils

2. **a.** Your teacher will give you a piece of drinking straw. Use a centimeter ruler to measure its length. Write its length here.

_____ cm

b. With your teacher's help, record the length of each student's straw.

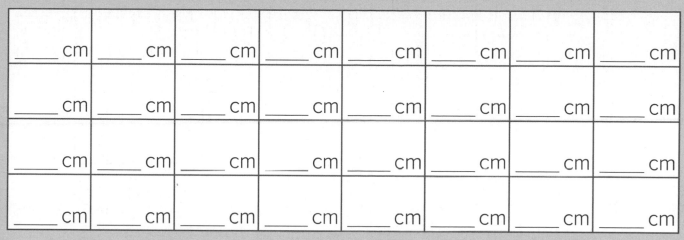

_____ cm	_____ cm	_____ cm	_____ cm	_____ cm	_____ cm	_____ cm	_____ cm
_____ cm	_____ cm	_____ cm	_____ cm	_____ cm	_____ cm	_____ cm	_____ cm
_____ cm	_____ cm	_____ cm	_____ cm	_____ cm	_____ cm	_____ cm	_____ cm
_____ cm	_____ cm	_____ cm	_____ cm	_____ cm	_____ cm	_____ cm	_____ cm

c. Use the measurements above to complete the line plot below. Show **your** measurement first.

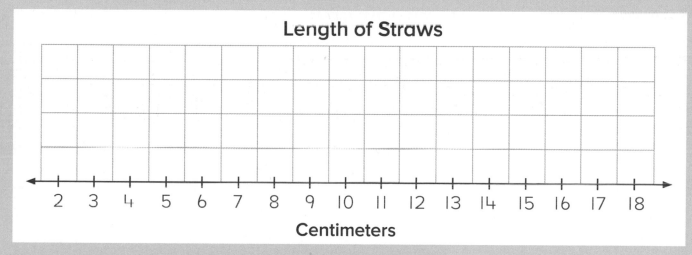

Length of Straws

2 3 4 5 6 7 8 9 10 11 12 13 14 15 16 17 18

Centimeters

d. What was the greatest length recorded?

e. What length or lengths occurred the most often?

Step Ahead

Draw a pencil that is longer than 10 centimeters but shorter than 5 inches.

Think and Solve Same shapes weigh the same. Write the missing value inside each shape.

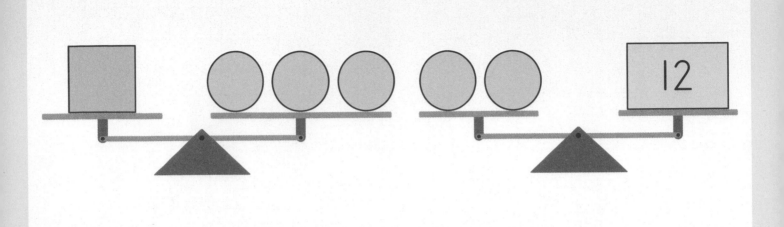

Words at Work

Choose and write words from the list to complete these sentences. One word is used more than once. One word is not used.

| hundreds |
| centimeter |
| zero |
| meter |
| tens |
| ones |

a. A _____ is shorter than one inch.

b. You should start at _____ when you measure with a ruler.

c. The number 415 can be split into four _____,

zero tens, and fifteen _____.

d. A ones block is one _____ long.

e. One _____ is a little bit longer than one yard.

Ongoing Practice

1. Write the matching time on the digital clock.

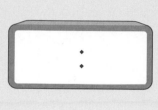

b.

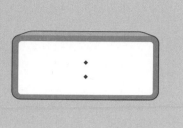

2. Three students threw paper airplanes.

a. For each, write the distance of the flight or color the bar graph to show the result.

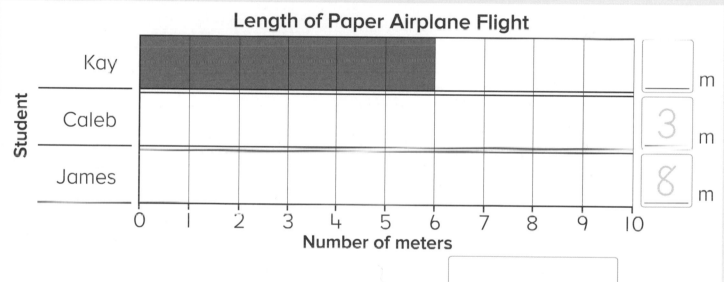

Length of Paper Airplane Flight

Kay _____ m

Caleb 3 m

James 8 m

Student

Number of meters

b. Who threw their plane the farthest? _____

c. How many meters did Kay's airplane fly? [___] _____ meters

Preparing for Module 10

Draw pictures to show how to regroup. Then complete the equation.

127 – 55 = [____]

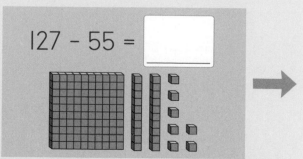

Step In

Noah has 224 cards in his collection. Mary has 20 fewer cards than Noah.

How many cards does Mary have?

> I figured out the answer in my head. I started at 224 and counted back by ones.

Max shows his thinking on a number line.

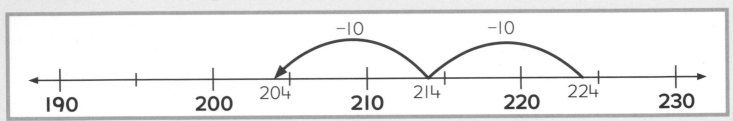

What steps does he follow?

Why does the number line start at 190 and not 0?

Use this number line to figure out 218 – 30. Draw jumps to show your thinking.

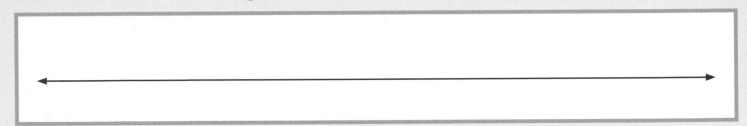

Step Up

1. Write each difference. Draw jumps on the number line to show your thinking.

a.

251 – 30 = _____

b.

344 – 20 = _____

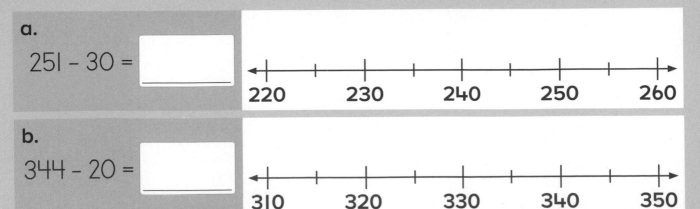

2. Write each difference. Show your thinking.

a.

$319 - 20 = $ ⬚

<--+----+----+----+----+----+----+----+----+----+-->
280   290   300   310   320

b.

$205 - 30 = $ ⬚

<--+----+----+----+----+----+----+----+----+----+-->
170   180   190   200   210

c.

$425 - 30 = $ ⬚

<--+----+----+----+----+----+----+----+----+----+-->
390   400   410   420   430

d.

$212 - 20 = $ ⬚

<--

e.

$304 - 10 = $ ⬚

<-->

f.

$415 - 30 = $ ⬚

<-->

Step Ahead Write the missing numbers along this trail.

305 → −30 → ⬚ → −20 → ⬚ → −30 → ⬚

⬚ ← −20 ← ⬚ ← −10 ← ⬚ ← −30 ←

Step In Jessica scored 285 points in a math game.
She scored 32 points more than her old record.

How could you figure out Jessica's old record?

Ryan figured out the difference on a number line.

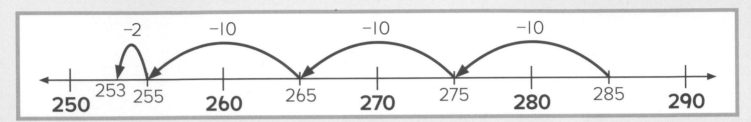

What steps did he follow?
How could you figure out the difference with fewer jumps?

Ricardo crossed out blocks to help figure out the difference.

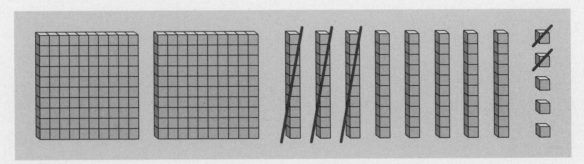

How many hundreds are left over? How many tens? How many ones?

Step Up 1. Write each difference. Draw jumps on the number line to show your thinking.

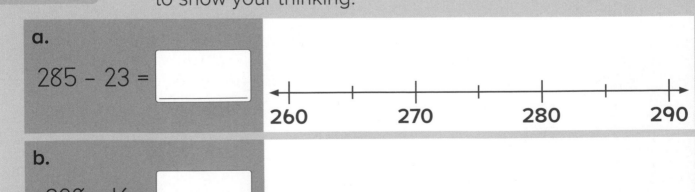

a.

$285 - 23 =$ ⬜

```
260      270      280      290
```

b.

$328 - 16 =$ ⬜

```
300      310      320      330
```

2. Write the number of hundreds, tens, and ones.
You can cross out blocks to help. Then write the difference.

a.

$345 - 13 = $ ___

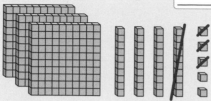

There are [3] hundreds.

There are [3] tens.

There are [2] ones.

b.

$458 - 25 = $ ___

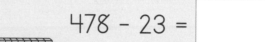

There are [ ] hundreds.

There are [ ] tens.

There are [ ] ones.

c.

$296 - 31 = $ ___

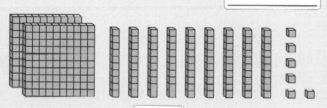

There are [ ] hundreds.

There are [ ] tens.

There are [ ] ones.

d.

$478 - 23 = $ ___

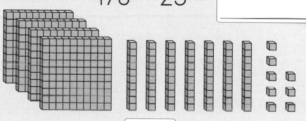

There are [ ] hundreds.

There are [ ] tens.

There are [ ] ones.

Step Ahead

Write an equation to match this number line.

___

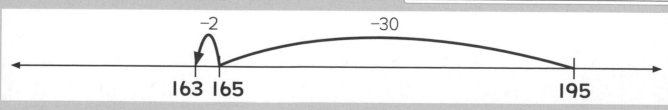

```
           −2              −30
      ╱╲ ╱‾‾‾‾‾‾‾‾‾‾‾‾‾‾‾╲
◄────┴──┴─────────────────┴────►
    163 165                195
```

Computation Practice   Why do horses wear shoes?

★ Complete the equation. Then write each letter above its matching answer at the bottom of the page.

20 + 69 = [ ] b   65 – 22 = [ ] i   75 – 8 = [ ] u

39 + 45 = [ ] w   28 + 31 = [ ] n   48 – 35 = [ ] c

87 – 64 = [ ] y   56 – 10 = [ ] o   61 + 37 = [ ] a

34 + 34 = [ ] d   25 – 14 = [ ] h   55 – 7 = [ ] t

18 + 23 = [ ] s   42 + 55 = [ ] e   95 – 24 = [ ] l

25 + 25 = [ ] k

 Some letters appear more than once.

89 97 13 98 67 41 97 48 11 97 23

84 46 67 71 68 71 46 46 50 41 43 71 71 23

84 43 48 11 41 46 13 50 41 46 59

I. Complete each equation. Show your thinking.

a.

47 + 18 = ☐

b.

59 + 28 = ☐

FROM 2.6.4

2. Write each difference. Draw jumps on the number line to show your thinking.

a.

132 – 10 = ☐

110   120   130   140

b.

185 – 20 = ☐

160   170   180   190

FFOM 2.10.1

Preparing for Module II

Show the position of the number on the number line. Then write the numbers that you will land on if you make jumps of 10.

a.

17

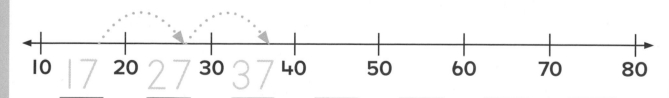

10   17   20   27   30   37   40   50   60   70   80

b.

34

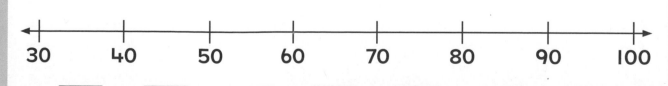

30   40   50   60   70   80   90   100

Step In A school art display raised $389 in ticket sales. $155 of this money was spent on prizes. How much money was left over?

How could you figure out the amount left over?

Valentina crossed out blocks to help figure out the difference.

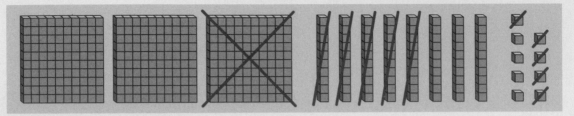

How many hundreds are left? How many tens? How many ones?

Victor drew a number line to help figure it out.

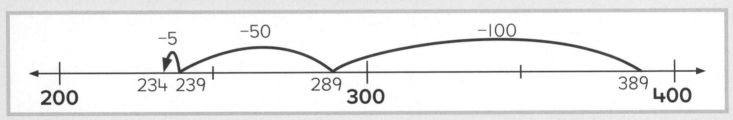

What number did he start with? How did he break up the other number?

Step Up

I. Write the number of hundreds, tens, and ones.
You can cross out blocks to help. Then write the difference.

a.
$$338 - 125 = \boxed{}$$

There are ☐ hundreds.

There are ☐ tens.

There are ☐ ones.

b.
$$428 - 212 = \boxed{}$$

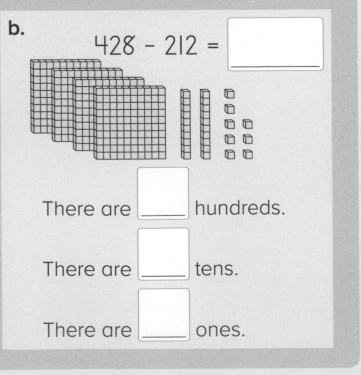

There are ☐ hundreds.

There are ☐ tens.

There are ☐ ones.

2. Draw jumps to show how you would figure out the difference. Then write the difference.

a. 485 – 132 = _____

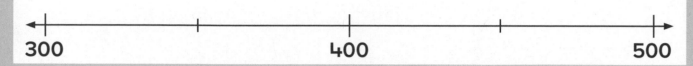

300   400   500

b. 877 – 116 = _____

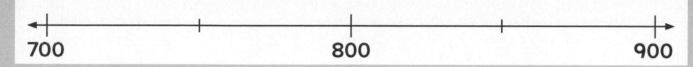

700   800   900

c. 659 – 132 = _____

d. 534 – 114 = _____

Step Ahead

Write an equation to match this number line.

_____

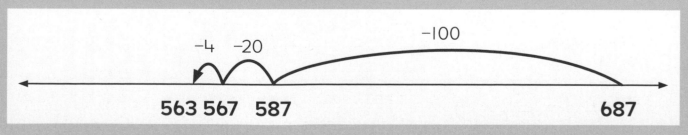

–4 –20   –100

563 567   587   687

Step In

How could you figure out the difference between these two prices?

$126

Charlie crossed out blocks to help figure out the difference.

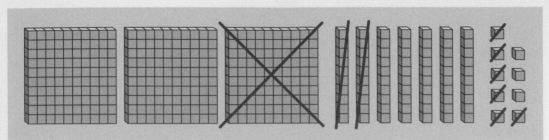

$379

Describe the steps that Charlie followed.

Abey used a number line to help find the difference.

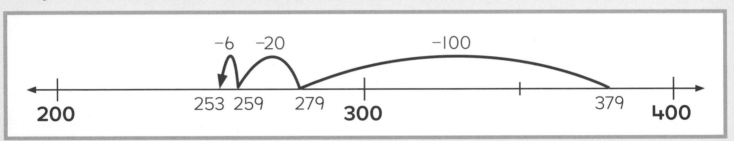

What steps did she follow?

How does she break the smaller number into parts to make it easier to subtract?

Step Up

1. Cross out hundreds, tens, and ones to figure out the difference. Then write the difference.

a.

287 − 52 = ☐

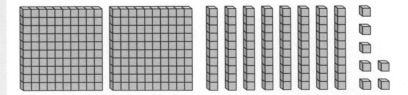

b.

358 − 135 = ☐

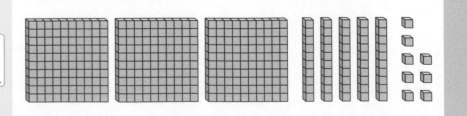

2. Write the difference. Draw jumps on the number line to show your thinking.

a. 374 – 63 = _____

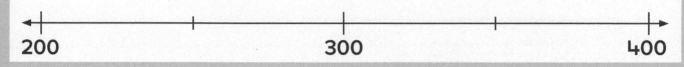

200   300   400

b. 759 – 106 = _____

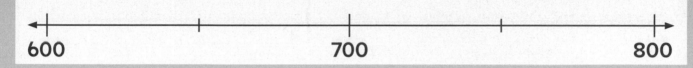

600   700   800

c. 586 – 142 – _____

d. 827 – 110 = _____

Step Ahead   Cody had $279 in the bank. He used some money to buy a game console for $135 and a set of controls for $27.

How much money does he have left in the bank? $_____

Think and Solve

Complete this magic square.

> In a magic square, the three numbers in each row, column, and diagonal add to make the same number. This is called the **magic number**.

The **magic number** is 18.

5		9
	6	
		7

Words at Work   Write about when you use subtraction outside of school.

_____

_____

_____

_____

_____

_____

_____

_____

_____

_____

1. Write the number of hundreds, tens, and ones. Then write an equation to show the total.

FROM 2.9.2

a. **532 + 26**

There are ⬛ 5 hundreds.

There are ⬛ 5 tens.

There are ⬛ 8 ones.

500 + _____ + _____ = _____

b. **245 + 32**

There are ⬛ hundreds.

There are ⬛ tens.

There are ⬛ ones.

_____ + _____ + _____ = _____

2. Draw jumps to show how you would figure out the difference. Then write the difference.

FRCM 2.10.3

679 – 154 = _____

```
+----+----+----+----+
500       600       700
```

How are these objects the same?

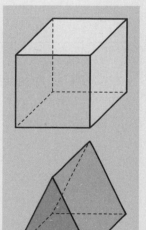

_____

_____

_____

Step In

Imagine you had **$349** in savings.
Which of these items could you buy?

How could you figure out how much money you would have left over?

Thomas chose the drums. He figured out $349 – $136 like this.

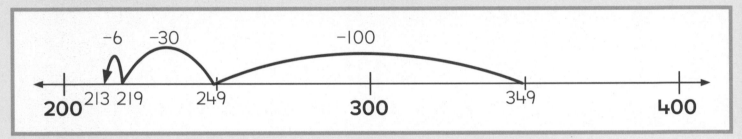

Janice chose the guitar. She figured out $349 – $235 like this.

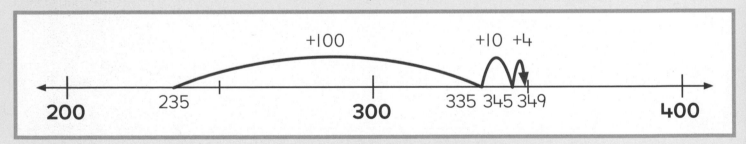

Why do you think they used different strategies for each problem?
How is the leftover amount of money shown on each number line?

Imagine you wanted to buy the keyboard.

Start at 349 and count on to 480 to figure out the amount you would
need to save.

I. Start at the larger number. Count back to take away the smaller number. Then write the difference.

a. 385 – 133 = _____

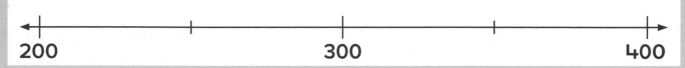

200　　　　　　　300　　　　　　　400

b. 792 – 121 = _____

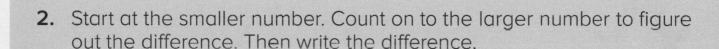

2. Start at the smaller number. Count on to the larger number to figure out the difference. Then write the difference.

a. 486 – 366 = _____

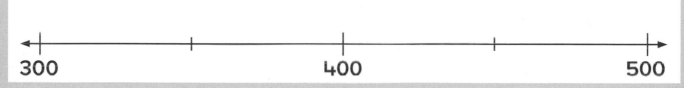

300　　　　　　　400　　　　　　　500

b. 689 – 578 = _____

Step Ahead

Layla has $745 in the bank.
She buys two speakers for $312 each.
How much money does she have left?

$_____

Working Space

Step In   Look at this picture of blocks.

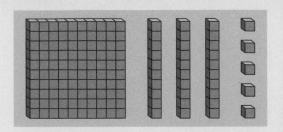

What number does it show?

What could you do with the blocks to make
14 ones blocks and keep the total the same?

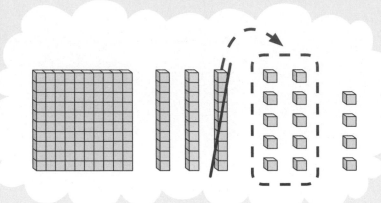

I could regroup 1 tens block as 10 ones blocks.
That makes 14 ones blocks and the total does not change.

Look at this picture of blocks.

What number does it show?

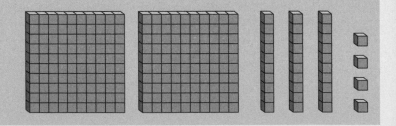

What could you do with the blocks to make 13 tens blocks
and keep the total the same?

How many hundreds blocks would you have left?

How many ones blocks would there be?

Does the total change?

1. Split each number into hundreds, tens, and ones.

a.
425 (is equal to) hundreds, tens, and ones

b.
382 (is equal to) ____ hundreds, ____ tens, and ____ ones

c.
697 (is equal to) ____ hundreds, ____ tens, and ____ ones

2. Complete these. Think carefully as there are many possible answers.

a.
265 is equal to   I hundred, ____ tens, and ____ ones

b.
283 is equal to   I hundred, ____ tens, and ____ ones

c.
326 is equal to   I hundred, ____ tens, and ____ ones

d.
613 is equal to   I hundred, ____ tens, and ____ ones

e.
437 is equal to   I hundred, ____ tens, and ____ ones

Step Ahead

Andrew is carrying a tray of hundreds, tens, and ones blocks. The blocks show the number 365. How many hundreds, tens, and ones blocks could be on the tray? Show three different ways.

____ hundreds, ____ tens, and ____ ones.

____ hundreds, ____ tens, and ____ ones.

____ hundreds, ____ tens, and ____ ones.

You can make notes on page 394 to help your thinking.

Computation Practice

★ Figure out each of these and use a ruler to draw a straight line to the matching difference. The line will pass through a number and a letter. Write each letter above its matching number at the bottom of the page.

The differences can be used more than once.

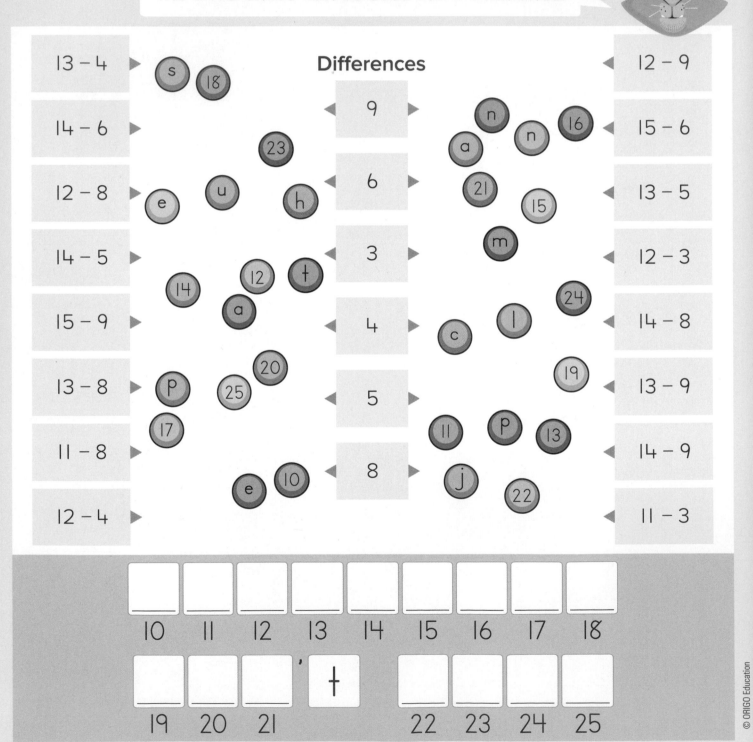

10	11	12	13	14	15	16	17	18

			t				
19	20	21		22	23	24	25

I. Draw jumps to show how you would figure out the total. Then write the total.

$437 + 28 =$ _____

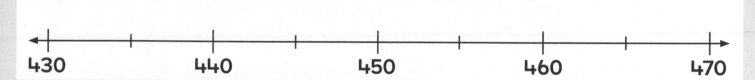

2. Count back to figure out the difference. Draw jumps to show your thinking.

a. $587 - 152 =$ _____

b. $485 - 151 =$ _____

Preparing for Module II   How are these objects the same?

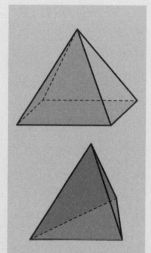

© ORIGO Education

FROM 2.9.6

FROM 2.10.5

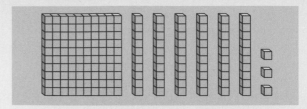

Step In Look at this picture of blocks.

What number does it show? _____

How would you change the blocks so that you could take away 5 ones blocks?

I need more ones, so I could regroup a tens block as 10 ones blocks. Then it is easy to take away the 5 ones. 163 - 5 = 158.

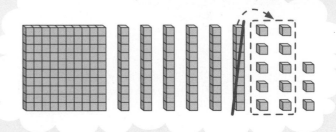

How would you figure out 163 – 5?

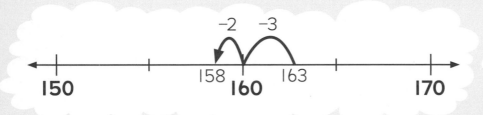

I could picture a number line and jump back 3 to 160 then 2 more to 158.

Step Up 1. Use blocks to help you subtract. Then write the difference.

a. 151 – 4 = _____

b. 276 – 8 = _____

c. 474 – 6 = _____

d. 345 – 8 = _____

e. 168 – 9 = _____

f. 593 – 5 = _____

© ORIGO Education

2. Draw jumps to show how you subtract. Then write the difference.

a.

$182 - 5 =$ [____]

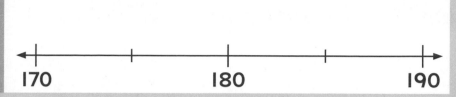

| | | | |
|170| |180| |190|

b.

$145 - 6 =$ [____]

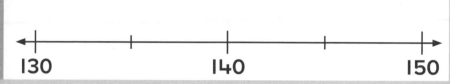

| | | | |
|130| |140| |150|

c.

$261 - 7 =$ [____]

(number line)

d.

$423 - 9 =$ [____]

(number line)

e.

$516 - 8 =$ [____]

(number line)

Step Ahead   Write the missing numbers along each trail.

a.

763 → −7 → [____] → −8 → [____] → −5 → [____] → −9 → [____]

b.

546 → −8 → [____] → −9 → [____] → −7 → [____] → −6 → [____]

© ORIGO Education

Step In Nancy has $216 in her savings.

If she buys this skateboard, how much money will she have left? How could you figure it out?

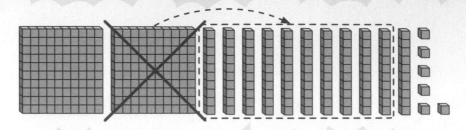

I would use blocks to show 216. I would have to regroup 1 hundreds block as 10 tens blocks. Then it's easy to figure out.

I would use a number line to subtract like this.

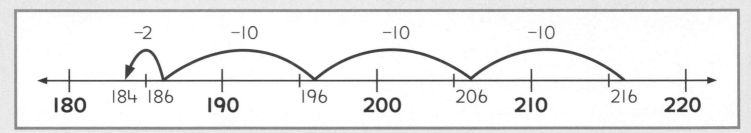

How would you figure out 253 – 26 using blocks?

How would you figure out 253 – 26 using a number line?

Step Up 1. Use blocks to help you subtract. Then write the difference.

a.
245 – 38 =

b.
157 – 29 =

c.
584 – 36 =

d.
423 – 32 =

e.
213 – 21 =

f.
426 – 34 =

2. Draw jumps to show how to figure out each of these. Then write the difference.

a.

$385 - 27 = \boxed{}$

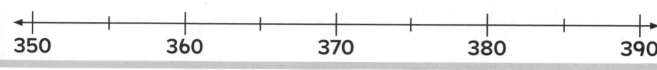

350   360   370   380   390

b.

$756 - 28 = \boxed{}$

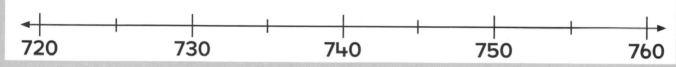

720   730   740   750   760

c.

$416 - 23 = \boxed{}$

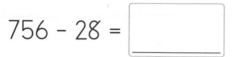

Step Ahead Solve the problem using blocks. Then show how you would solve the same problem on the number line.

$235 - 27 = \boxed{}$

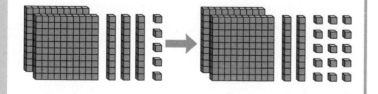

There are $\boxed{}$ hundreds

There are $\boxed{}$ tens.

There are $\boxed{}$ ones

Think and Solve Awan, Cathy, and Juan measured their heights.

Awan is 10 cm taller than Cathy.

Juan is 5 cm shorter than Cathy.

How much shorter is Juan than Awan?

[____] cm

Words at Work Write a subtraction equation that uses 328 and 67.

[____] – [____] = [____]

Write a word problem to match your equation.
Then write about how you figured out the answer.

© ORIGO Education

1. Use ones and tens blocks to measure each worm.

a.

[ ] centimeters long

FROM 2.9.9

b.

[ ] centimeters long

c.

[ ] centimeters long

2. Draw jumps to show how you subtract. Then write the difference.

a.

$164 - 7 =$ [ ]

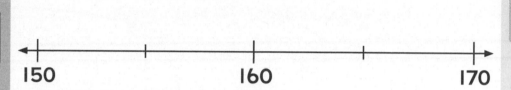

FROM 2.10.7

b.

$132 - 6 =$ [ ]

Preparing for Module 11   Draw a shape to match each label.

a.   a triangle with all sides
     a different length

b.   a quadrilateral with all sides
     the same length

Step In

What is the difference between the lengths of these reptiles?
How could you figure it out using a number line?

Komodo dragon 228 cm

Tokay gecko 33 cm

Teresa showed her thinking like this.

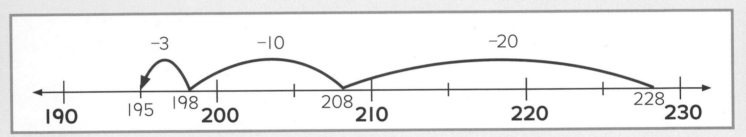

John showed his thinking like this.

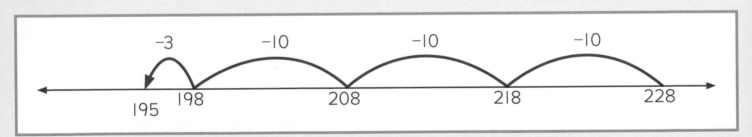

How could you use blocks to help you?

Step Up

1. Try thinking about these jumps in your head.
   Write the difference.

a. $324 - 20 - 2 = \underline{\hspace{2cm}}$

b. $547 - 20 - 4 = \underline{\hspace{2cm}}$

c. $738 - 30 - 4 = \underline{\hspace{2cm}}$

d. $625 - 20 - 10 = \underline{\hspace{2cm}}$

© ORIGO Education

2. Look at these tables about snakes and their lengths.

Snake	Length (cm)
Rosy Boa	105
Pine Snake	266
Scarlet Snake	32
Night Snake	27

Snake	Length (cm)
Ground Snake	21
Python	310
Rubber Boa	14
Anaconda	320

Try to figure out these in your head. You can use blocks or a number line if you need help.

a. How much longer is the Python than the Rubber Boa?

☐ – ☐ = ☐ cm

b. What is the difference in length between the Scarlet Snake and the Python?

☐ – ☐ = ☐ cm

c. How much longer is the Rosy Boa than the Ground Snake?

☐ – ☐ = ☐ cm

d. How much shorter is the Scarlet Snake than the Anaconda?

☐ – ☐ = ☐ cm

e. What is the difference in length between the Pine Snake and the Night Snake?

☐ – ☐ = ☐ cm

f. How much longer is the Anaconda than the Ground Snake?

☐ – ☐ = ☐ cm

Step Ahead

Look at the tables in Question 2 above. The total length of four of the snakes is greater than 400 cm but less than 500 cm. Which four snakes could this statement describe? There is more than one possible answer.

Step In Alejandro's family is going on vacation.

If they fly, it will cost $526 for plane tickets to their destination.
If they drive, it will cost $134 for the gas for their car.

How could you figure out the difference in cost?

I would picture a number line and subtract the hundreds, then the tens, then the ones.

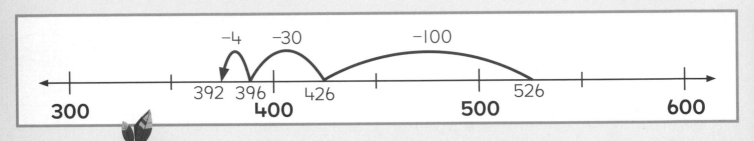

I would subtract the ones, then the tens, then the hundreds like this.

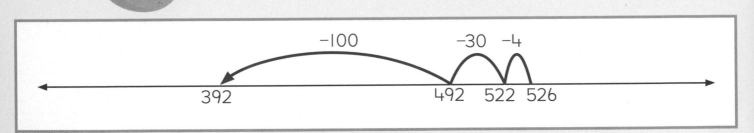

What do you notice about the difference for the two methods?

Step Up   1.   Use blocks to help you subtract. Then write the difference.

a.
264 – 127 =

b.
432 – 136 =

c.
543 – 138 =

d.
357 – 118 =

e.
228 – 135 =

f.
417 – 124 =

2. Draw jumps to show how you subtract. Then write the difference.

a.

364 – 119 = ☐

200   300   400

b.

592 – 126 = ☐

400   500   600

c.

829 – 134 = ☐

d.

504 – 132 = ☐

© ORIGO Education

Step Ahead   Oscar measured the heights of some people in his family.

Dad	Grandpa	Oscar	Damon	Riku
182 cm	163 cm	129 cm	112 cm	78 cm

a. What is the **least** difference in height? ☐ cm

b. Which two people had that difference?

Computation Practice   How many bones in the human body?

★ Complete the equations.
★ Then color all the parts below that show a difference that is **even**.

38 − 23 = ☐	65 − 55 = ☐	97 − 84 = ☐
74 − 62 = ☐	39 − 21 = ☐	28 − 17 = ☐
47 − 33 = ☐	57 − 41 = ☐	69 − 52 = ☐
89 − 83 = ☐	55 − 52 = ☐	99 − 91 = ☐
29 − 22 = ☐	82 − 71 = ☐	78 − 74 = ☐

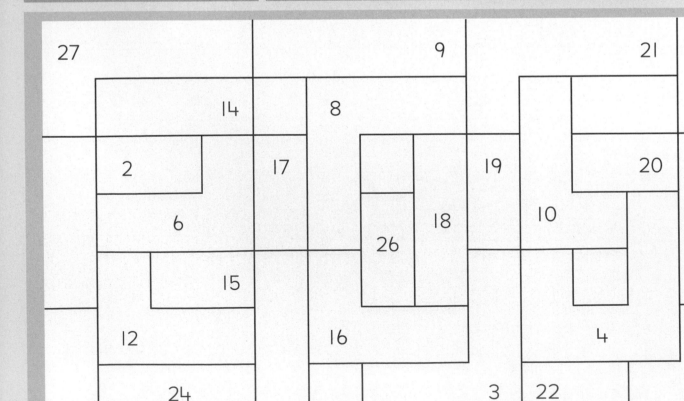

Ongoing Practice

1. Use a ruler to measure each object. Write the length in centimeters.

a.

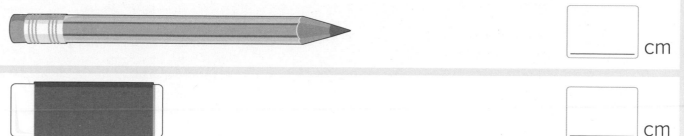

_____ cm

b.

_____ cm

2. Use the table to answer these.

Famous Tree	Height (ft)
Hyperion	379
General Sherman	275
Methuselah	208
Del Norte Titan	307

a. How much taller is the Hyperion than the Methuselah?

_____ − _____ = _____ ft

b. What is the difference in height between General Sherman and Del Norte Titan?

_____ − _____ = _____ ft

Preparing for Module II   Use skip counting to figure out the total amount.

a.

_____ cents

b.

_____ cents

Step In

How much more will it cost to buy the red guitar than the blue guitar?

$123

$108

How could you figure it out?

If you subtract, you make a very long jump. 123 - 100 - 8 = 15

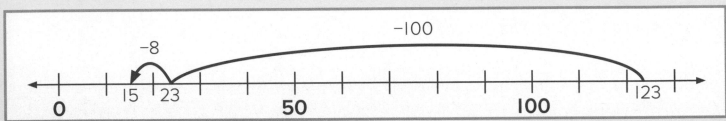

Sometimes it is easier to count on from the smaller number and add the jumps. 2 + 10 + 3 = 15

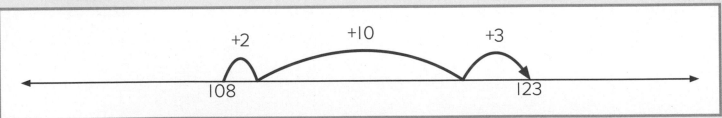

You could also count back to the smaller number like this. The difference is 15.

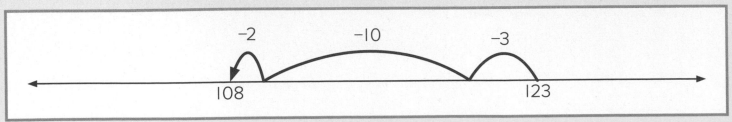

How would you figure out 156 – 128? Why?

© ORIGO Education

a.

212 – 131 = ☐

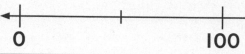

b.

184 – 127 = ☐

c.

275 – 108 = ☐

d.

232 – 116 = ☐

Step Ahead   Write the missing numbers along this trail.

506   ☐   ☐   ☐   ☐   ☐

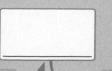 –100   +110   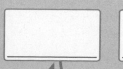 –120   +130   –20

Step In

These students figured out the number of days until they turned 8 years old. They recorded the number in this table.

Student	Number of Days
Ruby	165
Nathan	132
Laura	117
Carlos	285

How many fewer days did Laura record than Ruby?

What equations could you write to show your thinking?

I would start with 165 and subtract the hundreds, tens, and ones.
165 - 100 = 65
65 - 10 = 55
55 - 7 = 48

Or I could count on from 117.
117 + ③ = 120
120 + ㊵ = 160
160 + ⑤ = 165
and 40 + 5 + 3 = 48

How could you figure out the difference with blocks?

How could you find the difference on a number line?

Step Up

1. Look at the table above. Figure out the difference between the number of days for these students. Show your thinking by writing the steps you followed, drawing number lines, or using blocks.

a. Nathan and Ruby

Difference _____

b. Carlos and Nathan

Difference _____

2. Figure out each difference. Show your thinking.

a. 409 – 28 = [ ]

b. 745 – 117 = [ ]

c. 832 – 36 = [ ]

d. 208 – 135 = [ ]

Step Ahead   Each brick shows the total of the two bricks directly below. Write the missing numbers.

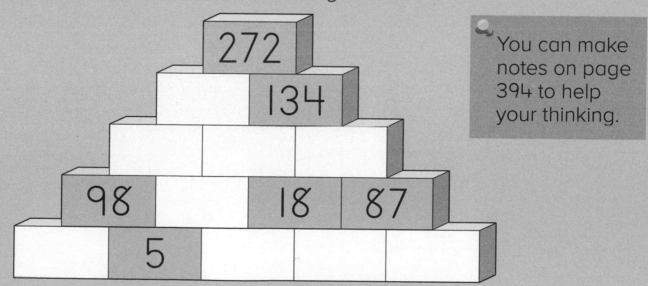

You can make notes on page 394 to help your thinking.

Think and Solve Follow the arrows and figure out the missing numbers in this pattern.

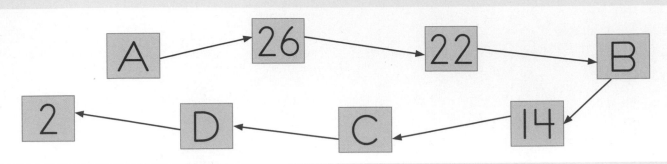

Write the numbers to complete these equations.

a. [A] + [B] = [ ]   b. [A] + [B] + [C] = [ ]

c. [A] + [B] + [C] − [D] = [ ]

Words at Work Write about the strategy you would use to solve this problem.

$275 - 189 = ?$

Ongoing Practice

1. Some students measured and recorded how high they could jump from a standing position. This line plot shows their measurements.

a. How many students recorded the highest jump?

_____ students

b. What was the shortest jump?

_____ cm

Standing Jumps

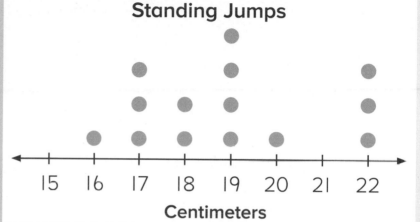

Centimeters

2. Figure out the difference. Draw jumps to show your thinking.

a.
245 – 164 = _____

0	100		200	300

b.
239 – 145 = _____

Preparing for Module 11

Color the coins you would use to pay the **exact** amount for each item.

a. 41¢

b. 36¢

Step In

Imagine you start at 0 and make jumps of 2 along this number line.

What numbers will you land on? How do you know?

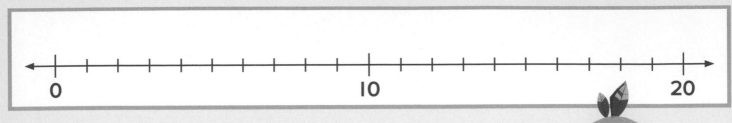

How many jumps will you make to reach 10?

5 steps of 2 is 10.

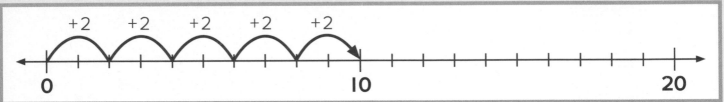

What equation could you write to match the jumps that you made?

2 + 2 + 2 + 2 + 2 = 10

Step Up

1. Complete each sentence. Use the number line above to help you.

a. **4** jumps of **2** is ☐

☐ + ☐ + ☐ + ☐ = ☐

b. **3** jumps of **2** is ☐

☐ + ☐ + ☐ = ☐

c. **7** jumps of **2** is ☐

☐ + ☐ + ☐ + ☐ + ☐ + ☐ + ☐ = ☐

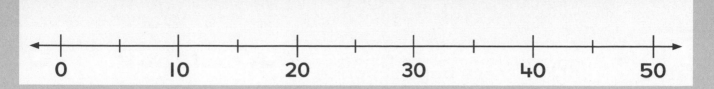

2. Complete these sentences. Use the number line above to help you.

a.
3 jumps of **5** is ☐

☐ + ☐ + ☐ = ☐

b.
4 jumps of **5** is ☐

☐ + ☐ + ☐ + ☐ = ☐

c.
6 jumps of **5** is ☐

☐ + ☐ + ☐ + ☐ + ☐ + ☐ = ☐

d.
8 jumps of **5** is ☐

☐ + ☐ + ☐ + ☐ + ☐ + ☐ + ☐ + ☐ = ☐

Step Ahead   **a.** Write the missing numbers.

2 + 2 + 2 + 2 + 2 = ____ | ____ jumps of ____ is ____

5 + 5 = ____ | ____ jumps of ____ is ____

b. Write what you notice.

_____

_____

Step In
Look at these bags of apples.

What do you notice?

How many bags are there?
How many apples are in each bag?

How could you figure out the total number of apples without counting each apple?

You could count in steps of 4. That's 4, 8, 12. 3 bags of 4 apples is 12 apples.

How could you arrange these apples into different equal groups?

You could make 2 bags of 6 apples.

Step Up
I. Write numbers to describe the equal groups.

a.

_____ bags of _____ is _____

b.

_____ boxes of _____ is _____

c.

_____ bunches of _____ is _____

d.
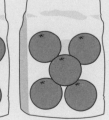

_____ packs of _____ is _____

2. Draw pictures to match. Then write the total.

a.

3 bags of 2 apples is ☐

b.

2 stacks of 5 blocks is ☐

c.

1 group of 4 people is ☐

d.

5 jars of 5 shells is ☐

Step Ahead

Arrange these boxes into equal groups. Complete the sentence. Draw a picture to show your thinking.

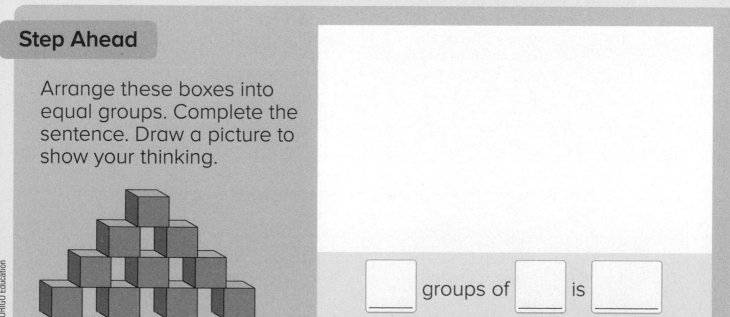

☐ groups of ☐ is ☐

© ORIGO Education

Computation Practice   What has many rings but no fingers?

★ Complete the equations.
★ Then color the letters that show each difference in the puzzle below.

65 – 36 =

49 – 31 =

85 – 46 =

97 – 64 =

58 – 42 =

98 – 22 =

56 – 21 =

75 – 19 =

39 – 17 =

95 – 68 =

Ongoing Practice

1. Write **P** inside each polygon. Then write the number of sides.

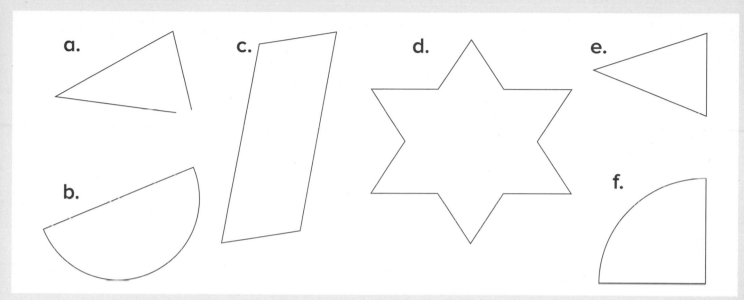

a.

b.

c.

d.

e.

f.

FROM 2.7.9

2. Write numbers to describe the equal groups.

a.

[ ] bunches of [ ] is [ ]

b.

[ ] bags of [ ] is [ ]

FROM 2.11.2

Preparing for Module 12

Color one part of each strip red.
Then write the fraction that is red.

a.

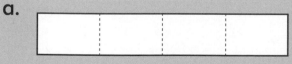

b.

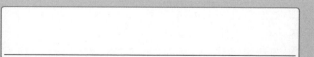

c.

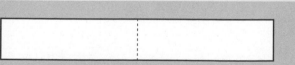

© ORIGO Education

Step In Look at these jars of marbles.

How many jars do you see? How many marbles in each jar?
How could you figure out the total number of marbles?

**What equation could you write
to show your thinking?**

Imagine there are four marbles in each jar.
What would be the total number of marbles? How do you know?

Step Up I. Write numbers to describe the equal groups.

a.

 groups of is

b.

groups of is

c.
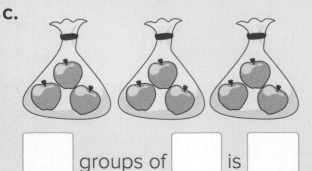

groups of is

d.
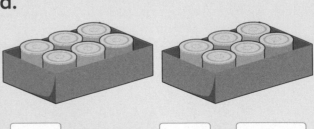

 groups of is

2. Write numbers to describe the equal groups.
Then write an equation to match.

a.

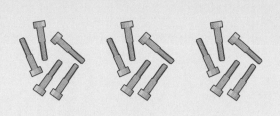

[ ] groups of [ ] is [ ]

[ ] + [ ] + [ ] = [ ]

b.

[ ] rows of [ ] is [ ]

[ ] + [ ] = [ ]

c.

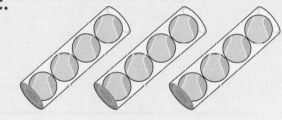

[ ] tubes of [ ] is [ ]

[ ] + [ ] + [ ] = [ ]

d.

[ ] stacks of [ ] is [ ]

[ ] + [ ] + [ ] + [ ] = [ ]

Step Ahead   Write the total. Then draw a picture to match the equation.

$8 + 8 + 8 =$ [ ]

Step In

Where are some places that you might see things arranged in rows?

An arrangement in rows with the same number in each row is called an **array**.

Look at this array of bugs.

How many rows of bugs are there?
How many bugs are in each row?

What is a number story you could tell to match the array?

A **row** goes across and a **column** goes up and down. Draw a line through each row in this picture.

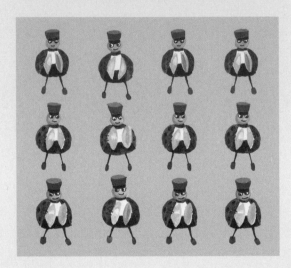

The bugs are marching in 3 rows. There are 4 bugs in each row.

Imagine another row of four bugs joined the band.

How many rows will there be? How many bugs will be in each row?
How many bugs will there be in total? How do you know?

Step Up

1. Write numbers to describe each array. Draw a line through each row to help you.

a.

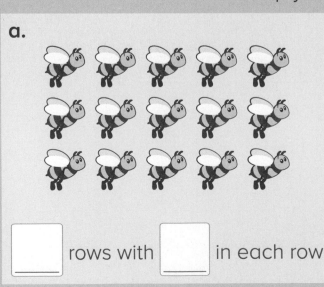

_____ rows with _____ in each row

b.

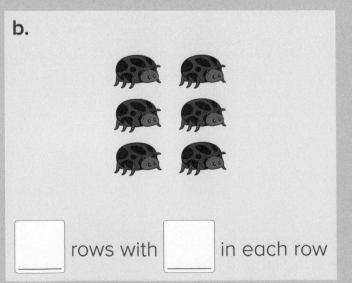

_____ rows with _____ in each row

2. Write the missing numbers.

a.

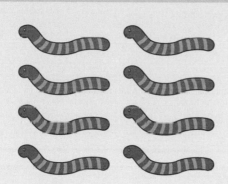

┌─────┐
│   │ rows
└─────┘

┌─────┐
│   │ in each row
└─────┘

b.

┌─────┐
│   │ rows
└─────┘

┌─────┐
│   │ in each row
└─────┘

c.

┌─────┐
│   │ rows
└─────┘

┌─────┐
│   │ in each row
└─────┘

d.

┌─────┐
│   │ rows
└─────┘

┌─────┐
│   │ in each row
└─────┘

Step Ahead Draw an array to match each story. Then circle the array that has more apples.

a. The apples are put in rows of 5. There are 3 rows.

b. The apples are put in rows of 4. There are 4 rows.

Think and Solve Imagine you threw two beanbags onto each target. Add the numbers in your head.

a. Write the greatest and least possible totals.

greatest   least

b. Write an equation to show one way you can make a **total of 30**.

☐ + ☐ + ☐ + ☐ = 30

c. Write an equation to show **one more way** to make a total of 30.

☐ + ☐ + ☐ + ☐ = 30

Words at Work   Imagine another student was away from school when you are learning about arrays. Write how you would describe an array to them.

Ongoing Practice   **1.** Draw these shapes.

FROM 2.7.12

a. a pentagon with three sides the same length

b. a quadrilateral with two sides the same length

2. Write numbers to describe each array.

FROM 2.11.4

a.

[ ] rows with [ ] in each row

b.

[ ] rows with [ ] in each row

Preparing for Module 12   Color one part of each shape red. Then circle the fraction that describes the colored part.

a.

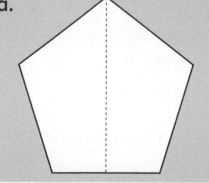

one-half   one-fourth

b.

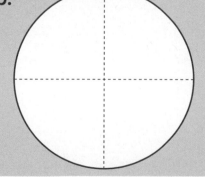

one-half   one-fourth

c.

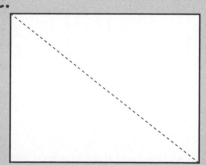

one-half   one-fourth

| Step In | Look at these bugs. |

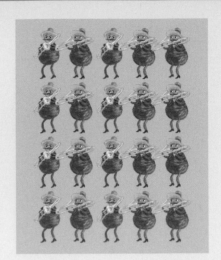

What is this type of arrangement called?

How many rows are there?
How many bugs in each row?

How could you find the total number of bugs?

What number story and equation could you write?

There are 4 rows with 5 bugs in each row.
That is 5 + 5 + 5 + 5 = 20.

| Step Up | I. Circle each row of bugs. Write the missing numbers. |

a.

[3] rows

[5] ladybugs in each row

[ ] + [ ] + [ ] = [ ]

b.

[ ] rows

[ ] ladybugs in each row

[ ] + [ ] = [ ]

c.

[ ] rows

[ ] ladybugs in each row

[ ] + [ ] + [ ] = [ ]

d.

[ ] rows

[ ] ladybugs in each row

[ ] + [ ] + [ ] = [ ]

2. Write a story to match each picture.

a.

_____
_____
_____

b.

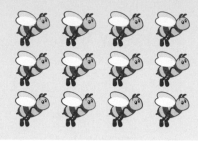

_____
_____
_____

c.

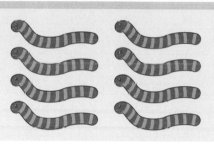

_____
_____
_____

d.

_____
_____
_____

Step Ahead

Draw an array of worms that has 5 rows. Then write a story **and** an equation to match.

_____
_____
_____
_____

Step In   What are some things that you know about 3D objects?

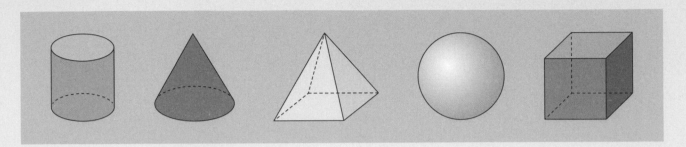

All 3D objects have surfaces.
Some objects have a flat surface.
A flat surface is called a **face**.

A 3D object with all flat faces is a **polyhedron**.

Look at the 3D objects at the top of the page.
Which objects are polyhedrons? How do you know?

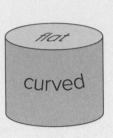 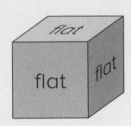

Step Up   1. Dixon was asked to shade **one face** red on each of these objects. Shade one ⬭ to describe his answer.

a.

- ⬭ He shaded a face.
- ⬭ He did not shade a face.

b.

- ⬭ He shaded a face.
- ⬭ He did not shade a face.

c.
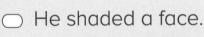
- ⬭ He shaded a face.
- ⬭ He did not shade a face.

d.
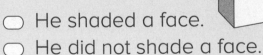
- ⬭ He shaded a face.
- ⬭ He did not shade a face.

e.

- ⬭ He shaded a face.
- ⬭ He did not shade a face.

f.
- ⬭ He shaded a face.
- ⬭ He did not shade a face.

2. Circle the polyhedrons.

a.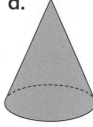

b.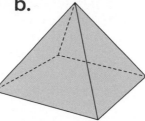

c.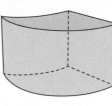

d.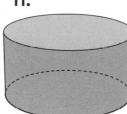

e.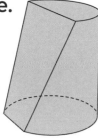

f.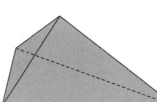

g.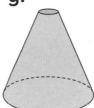

h.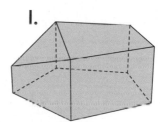

i.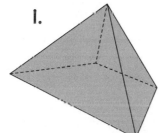

j.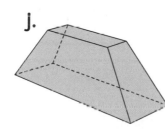

k.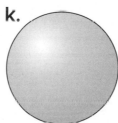

l.

Step Ahead   Write where you might see polyhedrons in your school.

Computation Practice

★ Complete these facts as fast as you can.

start | 14 − 7 = ☐ | 11 − 3 = ☐ | 12 − 6 = ☐

15 − 1 = ☐ | 13 − 2 = ☐ | 8 − 4 = ☐

10 − 6 = ☐ | 14 − 1 = ☐ | 12 − 3 = ☐

2 − 2 = ☐ | 8 − 1 = ☐ | 17 − 9 = ☐

12 − 5 = ☐ | 14 − 5 = ☐ | 12 − 4 = ☐

11 − 1 = ☐ | 6 − 3 = ☐ | 15 − 5 = ☐

18 − 9 = ☐ | 12 − 1 = ☐ | finish

1. Write the number to match. Show your thinking.

a. I hundred, 12 tens, and 5 ones

(is the same value as)

b. 2 hundreds, 5 tens, and 19 ones

(is the same value as)

2. Write a number story to match each picture.

a.

_____

_____

_____

b.

_____

_____

_____

Preparing for Module 12

Draw lines on each shape to show 4 equal parts. Then color **one-fourth**.

a.

b.

c.

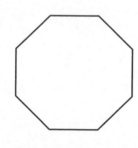

Step In

What are some things you know about pyramids?

A pyramid has many triangular faces that meet at a point.
The triangular faces all share one other face.

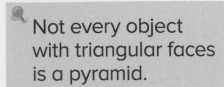
Not every object with triangular faces is a pyramid.

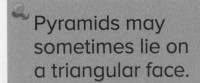
Pyramids may sometimes lie on a triangular face.

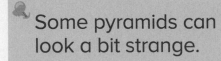
Some pyramids can look a bit strange.

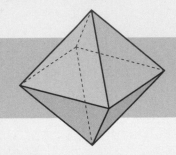

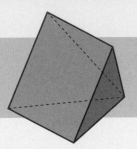

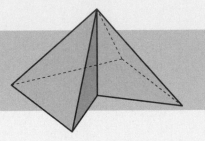

Where might you see pyramids?

Step Up

1. Look at each object. Count the number of triangular faces and write the total.

a.

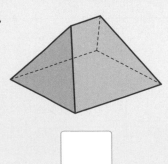

b.

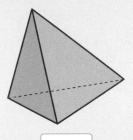

c.

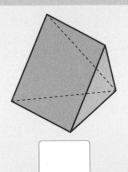

d.

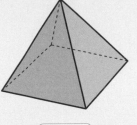

e.

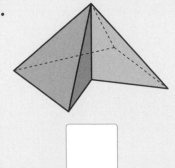

f.

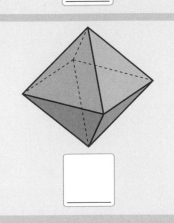

2. Circle the pyramids.

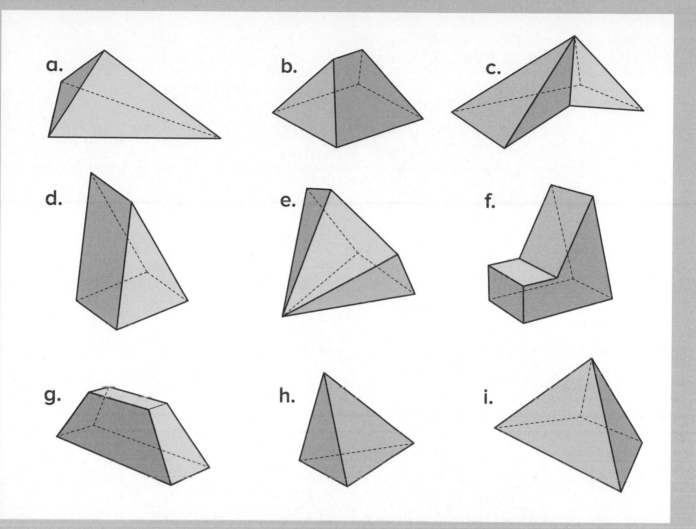

a.

b.

c.

d.

e.

f.

g.

h.

i.

Step Ahead

Step pyramids are buildings that are made up of layers of stone. They do not have smooth triangular faces like the pyramids above because the faces are actually steps.

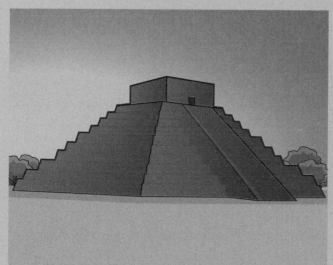

How many blocks have been used in the step pyramid below? Be sure to count the hidden blocks too.

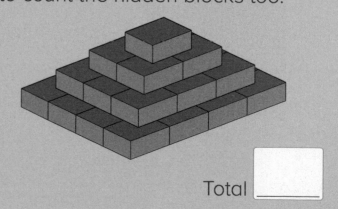

Total _____

Step In   Look at this object.

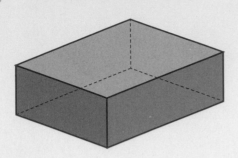

When two surfaces meet, they make an **edge**.

When three or more edges meet, they make a **vertex**. When there is more than one vertex, they are called **vertices**.

How many edges does this object have? How many vertices does it have?

Look at this cylinder.

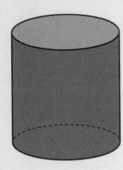

How many edges does this cylinder have? How do you know?

How many vertices does it have? How do you know?

How is the cylinder different from the first object?
How is it the same?

Step Up   1. Complete the chart. Use real objects to help you count the vertices, edges, and faces.

Object	Vertices	Straight edges	Curved edges	Flat faces	Curved surfaces
a.	8				
b.		0			

2. Complete this chart.

Object	Vertices	Straight edges	Curved edges	Flat faces	Curved surfaces
a.					
b.	8				
c.					

Step Ahead   Imagine you sliced a corner off a cube. Complete this table.

	Large piece	Small piece
Number of edges		
Number of vertices		
Number of faces		

© ORIGO Education

Think and Solve Use the shapes to draw a picture that costs $30.

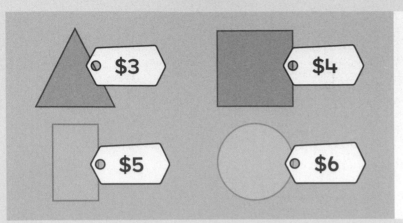

Words at Work Write the answer for each clue in the grid. Use words from the list.

Clues Across	Clues Down
1. A pyramid has three or more triangular faces that meet at one __.	**2.** When __ or more edges meet, they make a vertex.
3. A flat surface on a 3D object is called a __.	**3.** A polyhedron is a 3D object with all __ faces.
5. An __ has the same number of things in each row.	**4.** When two surfaces meet, they make an __.
6. Three bags of three pears is __ pears.	

face
edge
nine
three
array
flat
point

Ongoing Practice

1. Show the position of each number. You can break the number line into more parts to help your thinking.

a.

45

0 ————————————————————→ 100

b.

63

0 ————————————————————→ 100

2. Circle the objects that are **not** pyramids.

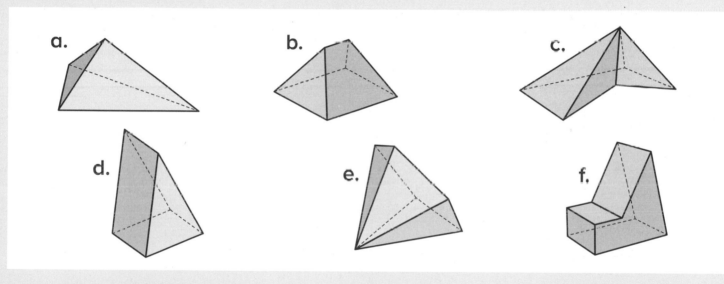

a.

b.

c.

d.

e.

f.

Preparing for Module 12   Circle the shapes that show one-fourth purple.

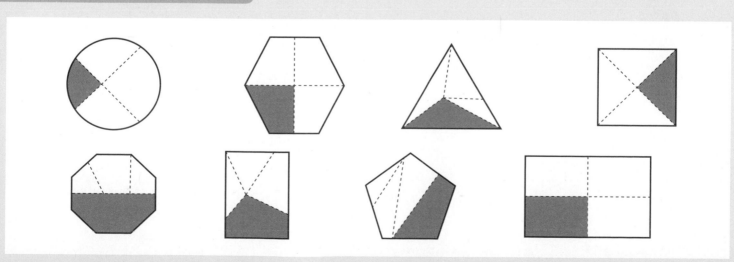

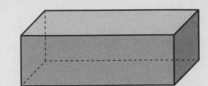

Step In   Imagine you had to draw this box.

Do you think it would be easy or hard? Why?

Try using this method to draw boxes.

a. Draw a non-square rectangle.	
b. Above and to one side of the first non-square rectangle, draw a second one the same size.	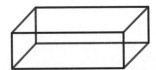
c. Connect matching vertices (such as top-left to top-left).	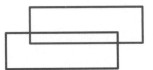

Step Up   **1.** Use the method above to copy these drawings. The face closest to you is blue.

a.

b.

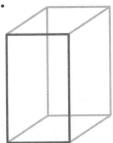

2. Use the same method to draw four boxes that your teacher will give you. Think carefully about which face you will draw first.

a.

b.

c.

d.

Step Ahead

Copy this picture using the same drawing method.

Step In   Look at these coins.

What is the name of each coin?
How much is each coin worth?

Sometimes these types of coins show different pictures.
Why do they show different pictures? What different pictures have you seen?

What is shown on the right?

What is its value in dollars?
What is its value in cents?
How many dimes could you trade for one dollar?
How do you know?
How many nickels could you trade for one dollar?

Step Up   I.   Write the missing numbers.

a.

4 dimes is _40_ ¢

2 nickels is _10_ ¢

3 pennies is _3_ ¢

The total is _53_ ¢

b.

2 quarters is _50_ ¢

3 dimes is _30_ ¢

I nickel is _5_ ¢

The total is _85_ ¢

2. Circle together the coins that equal one dollar.
Then write the total amount.

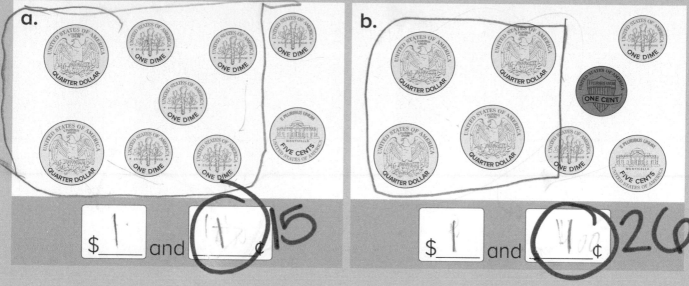

a.

$__1__ and __15__¢ ⟨15⟩

b.

$__1__ and __26__¢ ⟨26⟩

3. Read the story. Write the missing numbers.

Gavin had 4 quarters, 2 dimes, and 3 nickels in his wallet.

He had __1__ dollar and __35__ cents. ⟨35⟩ ✓

Gavin gave his sister a dime. Then he found a quarter on the sidewalk.

Now Gavin has __1__ dollar and __50__ cents. ⟨50⟩

Step Ahead

Peta has 4 coins in her pocket. The total is greater than 40 cents but less than 60 cents. Draw two different pictures to show the coins she might have in her pocket.

50¢   49¢

1¢

5¢

10¢

25¢

Computation Practice   What do dragonflies eat?

★ Complete the equations. Then write each letter above its matching answer at the bottom of the page.

65 – 19 = ☐ a   57 – 36 = ☐ f   25 + 25 = ☐ s

96 – 45 = ☐ n   72 – 35 = ☐ d   58 + 13 = ☐ l

34 + 34 = ☐ o   35 – 18 = ☐ e   74 – 52 = ☐ u

32 + 32 = ☐ r   85 – 49 = ☐ g   49 + 23 = ☐ t

62 + 26 = ☐ i   75 – 28 = ☐ q   87 – 32 = ☐ m

Some letters appear more than once.

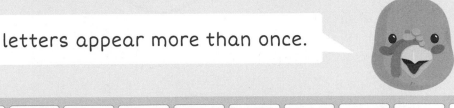

☐ ☐ ☐ ☐ ☐ ☐ ☐ ☐ ☐ ☐ ☐
37 64 46 36 68 51 21 71 88 17 50

☐ ☐ ☐
17 46 72

☐ ☐ ☐ ☐ ☐ ☐ ☐ ☐ ☐ ☐
55 68 50 47 22 88 72 68 17 50

1. Draw jumps to show how you would figure out these. Then write the differences.

a.

475 – 127 = ☐

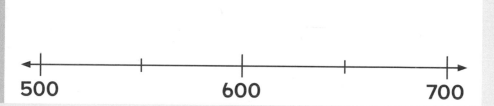

300   400   500

b.

651 – 135 = ☐

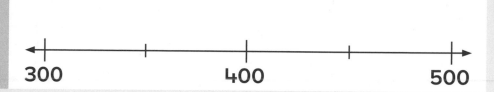

500   600   700

2. Circle together the coins that equal one dollar. Then write the total amount.

a.

$_____ and _____¢

b

$_____ and _____¢

Preparing for Module 12

Write the number of cubes. Then color ◯ beside the words that best describe the weight of the toy.

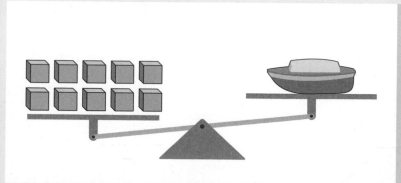

◯ more than ☐ cubes

◯ less than ☐ cubes

◯ the same as ☐ cubes

Step In Look at the coins and fruit below.

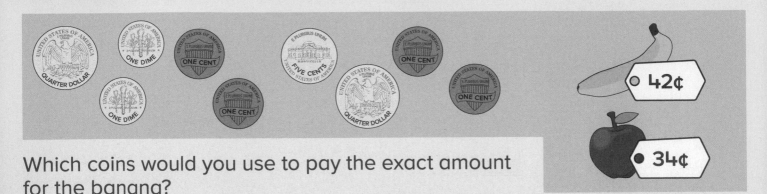

Which coins would you use to pay the exact amount for the banana?

Which coins could you use to pay for the banana and get some change?

Which coins would you use to pay for the apple? Why?

Imagine you had these bills.

Would you have more than or less than $30?

How did you figure it out?

Step Up I. Write or draw two different ways to pay for each fruit using nickels, dimes, and quarters. Use exact amounts because **no change will be given**.

5¢ 10¢ 25¢

a.  45¢ each   25¢ 10¢ 10¢
_____

b.  30¢ each
_____

2. Use tallies to show two different ways to pay for each item.
Use exact amounts because **no change will be given**.

a.

$28

10 dollars	5 dollars	1 dollar
II	I	III

b.

$23

10 dollars	5 dollars	1 dollar

3. Use tallies to show how to pay for each item.
Use amounts that will give you just a few dollars change.

a.

$68

10 dollars	5 dollars

b.

SPACE
ADVENTURE

$44

10 dollars	5 dollars

© ORIGO Education

Step Ahead

Sheree has one dollar, one quarter, three dimes, and two nickels.

a. If she traded all the money for pennies, how many pennies would she have?

b. If she traded all the money for nickels, how many nickels would she have?

Step In   Would you rather have a $1 bill or six coins? Why?

If the coins were not worth much, I would rather have the dollar bill.

If some of the coins were quarters, the total of the coins might be worth more than one dollar.

Imagine you could only have three of one type of coin and three of another.

Would you rather have these coins or a $1 bill? How did you decide?

Step Up   1.   Write the total.

a.

The total is $ _____ and _____ ¢.

b.

The total is $ _____ and _____ ¢.

2. Solve each problem. Show your thinking.

a. David had two $1 bills and 3 quarters in his wallet. Then he found another 2 quarters in his pocket. How much money does he have in total now?

$_____ and _____¢

b. Daniela has 74 cents and Felipe has 2 dimes, a quarter, and a nickel. If they combine their money, how much will they have in total?

$_____ and _____¢

c. Stella had some money in her money box. She put in 5 dimes and 3 nickels. Now she has $2 and 80 cents. How much was in her money box before?

$_____ and _____¢

d. William has 5 quarters fewer than Nicole. William has 6 quarters. How much money does Nicole have?

$_____ and _____¢

Step Ahead

Sumi has a $1 bill and 2 coins in her pocket.

a. What could be the greatest amount in her pocket?

b. What could be the least amount? _____

Think and Solve   Same shapes weigh the same. Write the missing value inside each shape.

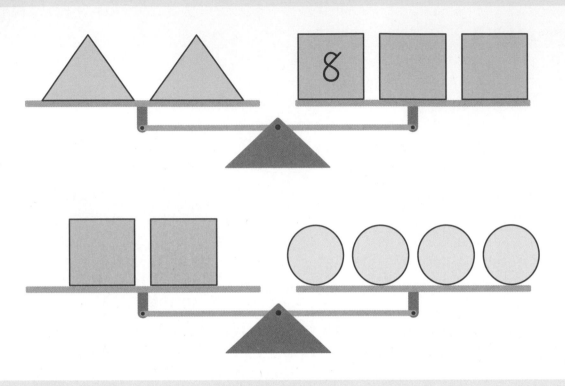

Words at Work   Write in words how you solve this problem.

Ethan has one bill and 5 coins that are each less than 50 cents.
What is the greatest amount of money he could have?
What is the least amount of money he could have?

Ongoing Practice

1. Figure out each difference. Show your thinking.

a.
307 – 24 = ☐

b.
246 – 135 = ☐

2. Use tallies to show one way to pay for the item.
Use the exact amount because **no change will be given**.

Preparing for Module 12

Write the number of medicine cups that fill each container.

Container	Number of Medicine Cups	
a.		☐ medicine cups
b.		☐ medicine cups
c.		☐ medicine cups

© ORIGO Education

Step In   Look at this picture of fruit.

Which fruit could you equally share among the three bears without cutting any pieces? How do you know?

How many apples will each bear receive? How do you know?
How many pears will each bear receive? How do you know?

Which fruit cannot be shared equally by three?
How many will be left over?

Step Up   **1.**   Your teacher will give you a sharing mat. Use cubes on the mat to figure out each share. Then complete the sentence.

a. There are 12 🍎 in total.

There are 3 bags.

There are _____ 🍎 in each bag.

b. There are 18 🍐 in total.

There are 3 plates.

There are _____ 🍐 on each plate.

c. There are 30 🍓 in total.

There are 3 bowls.

There are _____ 🍓 in each bowl.

d. There are 24 🍌 in total.

There are 3 bunches.

There are _____ 🍌 in each bunch.

e. There are 24 🍊 in total.

There are 4 packs.

There are _____ 🍊 in each pack.

f. There are 28 🫐 in total.

There are 4 bowls.

There are _____ 🫐 in each bowl.

2. Complete each of these.

a. There are 20 🍒 in total.

There are 4 plates.

There are _____ 🍒 on each plate.

b. There are 16 🍇 in total.

There are 4 bowls.

There are _____ 🍇 on each bowl.

c. There are 32 ● in total.

There are 4 cans.

There are _____ ● in each can.

d. There are 4 🍊 in total.

There are 4 bowls.

There is _____ 🍊 in each bowl.

3. Write the number in each group.

a.

GOLF BALLS   GOLF BALLS   GOLF BALLS

| 12 | balls | 3 | packs |

_____ balls in each pack

b.

BLOCKS BLOCKS BLOCKS BLOCKS

| 16 | blocks | 4 | boxes |

_____ blocks in each box

Step Ahead

Jamal needs to share these marbles among five friends — not four. How can he share the marbles so that each friend will have the same number?

_____

_____

_____

_____

Step In   These 12 dinosaurs like to dance in equal groups.

Imagine the dinosaurs danced in groups of 3.
How many groups would there be? How do you know?

Imagine the dinosaurs danced in groups of 2.
How many groups would there be? How do you know?

What other numbers could be in each equal group?
How many groups would there be?

Step Up   1. Your teacher will give you a grouping mat. Use cubes
on the mat to figure out the equal groups. Then complete
the sentence.

a.
There are 12 🦕 in total.

There are 3 🦕 in each group.

There are _____ groups.

b.
There are 15 🦖 in total.

There are 3 🦖 in each group.

There are _____ groups.

c.
There are 24 🦕 in total.

There are 2 🦕 in each group.

There are _____ groups.

d.
There are 16 🦕 in total.

There are 4 🦕 in each group.

There are _____ groups.

© ORIGO Education

2. Complete each sentence.

a. There are 18 🥚 in total.

There are 6 🥚 in each nest.

There are _____ nests.

b. There are 25 🥚 in total.

There are 5 🥚 in each nest.

There are _____ nests.

c. There are 7 🥚 in total.

There is 1 🥚 in each nest.

There are _____ nests.

d. There are 21 🥚 in total.

There are 7 🥚 in each nest.

There are _____ nests.

3. Write a word story to match this picture of dinosaur eggs.

_____

_____

_____

_____

Step Ahead

Twenty dinosaurs dance in equal groups. How many groups could there be? How many would be in each group? Write numbers to complete possible answers.

1	group	20	in each group
[ ]	groups	[ ]	in each group
[ ]	groups	[ ]	in each group

[ ]	groups	[ ]	in each group
[ ]	groups	[ ]	in each group
[ ]	groups	[ ]	in each group

Computation Practice

What goes from Baltimore to New York but never moves?

★ Complete the equations. Then find each total in the puzzle below and color its matching letter.

62 + 19 = ☐	57 + 34 = ☐	35 + 24 = ☐
21 + 47 = ☐	15 + 14 = ☐	42 + 36 = ☐
45 + 48 = ☐	23 + 56 = ☐	23 + 66 = ☐
36 + 18 = ☐	29 + 28 = ☐	16 + 49 = ☐
57 + 18 = ☐	35 + 41 = ☐	

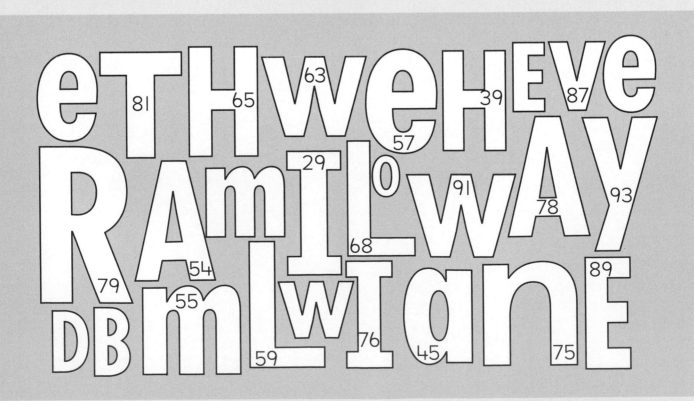

ORIGO Stepping Stones • Grade 2 • 12.2

© ORIGO Education

Ongoing Practice

1. Complete each sentence.

a.
3 jumps of 2 is [ ]

[ ] + [ ] + [ ] = [ ]

b.
2 jumps of 2 is [ ]

[ ] + [ ] = [ ]

c.
6 jumps of 2 is [ ]

[ ] + [ ] + [ ] + [ ] + [ ] + [ ] = [ ]

2. Complete each of these. You can use cubes on a sharing mat to help.

a. There are 12 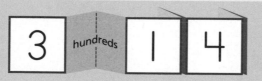 in total.

There are 4 plates.

I here are _____ 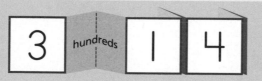 on each plate.

b. There are 8 ⬤ in total.

There are 4 bags.

I here are _____ ⬤ in each bag.

Preparing for Next Year

Look at the number on the expander. Then write the matching numeral and complete the number name.

a.

| 3 | hundreds | 1 | 4 |

[ ]

_____ hundred _____

b.

| 6 | hundreds | 0 | 7 |

[ ]

_____ hundred _____

Step In What do you notice about each of these shapes?

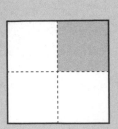 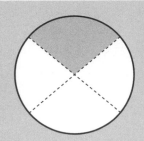 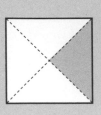

How would you describe the amount that is shaded?

What fraction name would you say?

> These shapes have all been split into four equal parts. One part of each shape is shaded, so each shape shows one-fourth.

Shade one part of the shape on the right.

How could you describe the amount that is shaded?

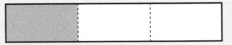

> Fraction names like third and fourth are the same as the names used to describe order but they have a different meaning with fractions.

Step Up 1. Color one part of each shape. Then write the name of the fraction that is shaded.

a.
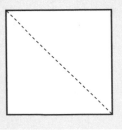

b.
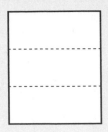

c.
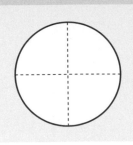

2. Beside each fraction name write the picture that matches. Some names match more than one picture. Some pictures have no match.

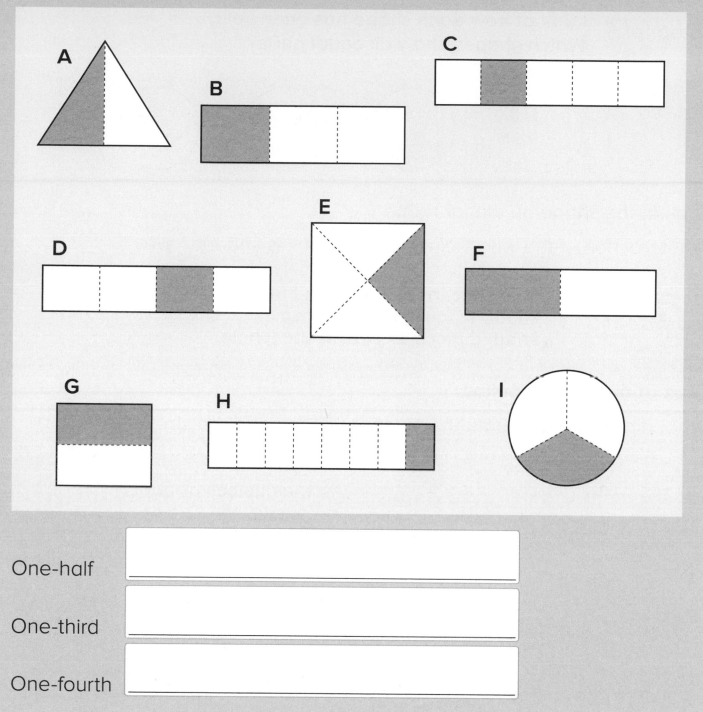

One-half

One-third

One-fourth

Step Ahead   Color the picture to help solve the problem.

Trina ate one-fourth of the pizza.

How many pieces are left?   ____ pieces

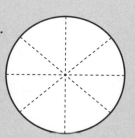

Step In

Look at how each shape has been split.
Which shapes show all equal parts?

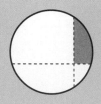  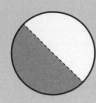 

Look at the shape on the far right.

What fraction of the whole circle do you think is shaded? Why?

It is split into two parts but they aren't equal. It looks like four copies of the shaded piece would fill the whole.

Look at the shapes below.

What do you notice about the number of parts and the size of each part?

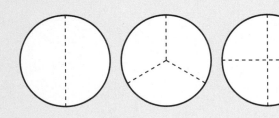

As the number of parts increases, the size of each part decreases.

Step Up

I. Circle the pictures that have been divided into parts of equal size.

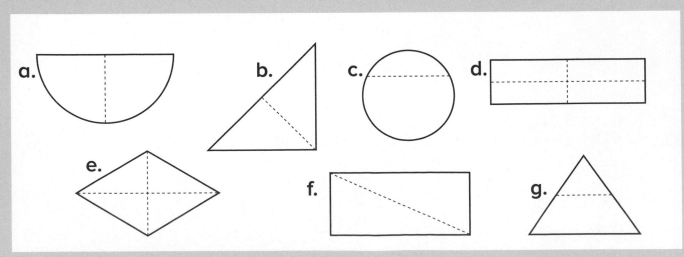

2. Circle the shapes that show **one-half** shaded.

a.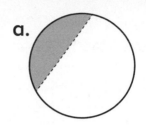

b.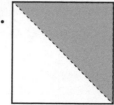

c.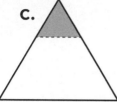

d.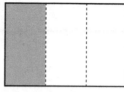

e.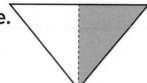

f.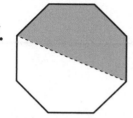

3. Color one part in each strip. Then circle the strips that show **one-fourth** shaded.

a.

b.

c.

d.

Step Ahead   Fold a sheet of paper in half, then in half and half again.

a. After each fold, write the number of parts of equal size.

   I fold = 2 parts

   2 folds = ⬜ parts

   3 folds = ⬜ parts

b. What pattern do you see?

© ORIGO Education

Think and Solve

For each square, add the numbers in the **shaded boxes** to figure out the **magic number.** Complete each magic square.

In a magic square, the three numbers in each row, column, and diagonal add to make the same number. This is called the **magic number.**

a.

3	8	
	4	6
7	0	

b.

9		7
	10	
13		11

Words at Work

Write about all the different ways you could split 12 eggs into equal groups. Explain your thinking.

Ongoing Practice

1. Write numbers to describe the equal groups.
Then write an addition sentence to match.

FROM 2.11.3

a.

_____ groups of _____ is _____

_____ + _____ + _____ + _____ = _____

b.

_____ rows of _____ is _____

_____ + _____ = _____

2. Complete each sentence.

FROM 2.12.2

a. There are 12 🥚 in total.

There are 3 🥚 in each nest.

There are _____ nests.

b. There are 20 🥚 in total.

There are 4 🥚 in each nest.

There are _____ nests.

c. There are 15 🥚 in total.

There are 5 🥚 in each nest.

There are _____ nests.

d. There are 21 🥚 in total.

There are 3 🥚 in each nest.

There are _____ nests.

Preparing for Next Year

Write the number that should be in the position shown by each arrow.

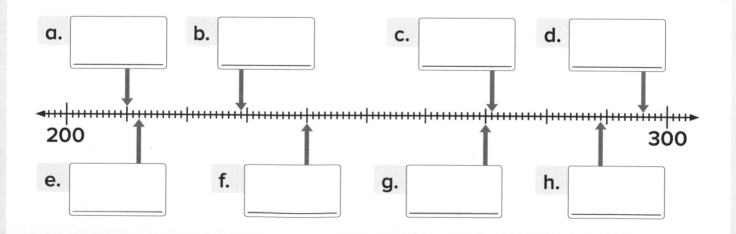

a. [ ] b. [ ] c. [ ] d. [ ]

200   300

e. [ ] f. [ ] g. [ ] h. [ ]

Step In   Imagine you cut each sandwich in half to share with a friend.

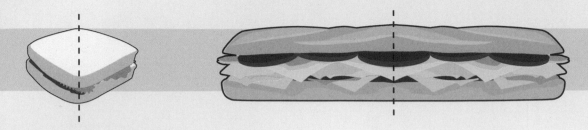

Compare the halves of each sandwich.
What is the same? What is different?

Each sandwich shows
two parts the same size.

One-half of one sandwich is less than
one-half of the other sandwich.

**Imagine Sara had 12 marbles in a bag and gave one-half to Mary.
Isaac had 18 marbles in a bag and gave one-half to Jack.**

Now Mary and Jack both have one-half of a bag of marbles.
Do they have the same number of marbles? How do you know?

Does one-half always show the same quantity or amount?

Step Up   I.   Color **one-half** of each picture.

a.

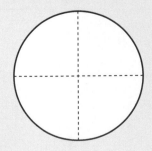

b.

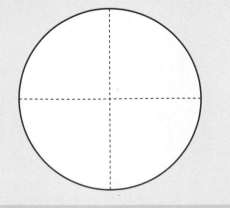

2. Draw straight lines to show each shape split into the fractions shown. Try to split each shape in the same way. Then color one part of each shape.

Halves

a.   b. 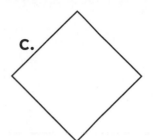 c. 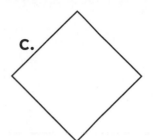 d.

Thirds

e.   f.   g. 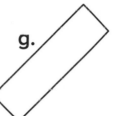 h.

Fourths

i.  j. 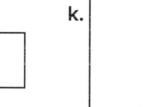 k.   l.

Step Ahead Color parts in the last picture to continue the pattern.

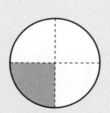  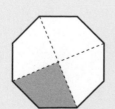 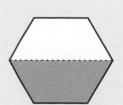 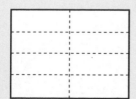

Step In

Look at these pictures.
What amount of each shape is shaded?

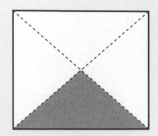 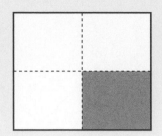 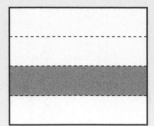

What do you notice about each fraction?
What is the same? What is different?

Each shape shows the same fraction.

The shape of the parts is different.

What is another way you could show the same fraction?

Step Up

1. Draw lines to join each fraction picture with a matching name.

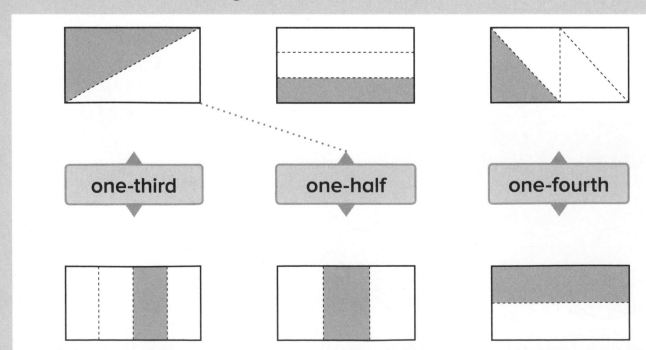

one-third   one-half   one-fourth

2. Use a ruler to draw straight lines that show each shape split into the fractions shown. Make the splits different for each pair of shapes.

a. Halves

b. Fourths

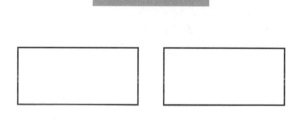

c. Thirds

d. Fourths

e. Halves

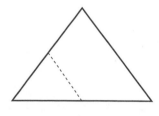

f. Thirds

Step Ahead   Draw more lines to divide each of these into parts of equal size.

a.

b.

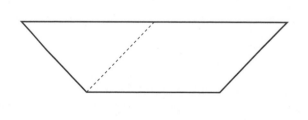

Computation Practice

Where would you work if you made faces all day?

★ Complete the equations. Then write each letter above its matching difference at the bottom of the page. Some letters appear more than once.

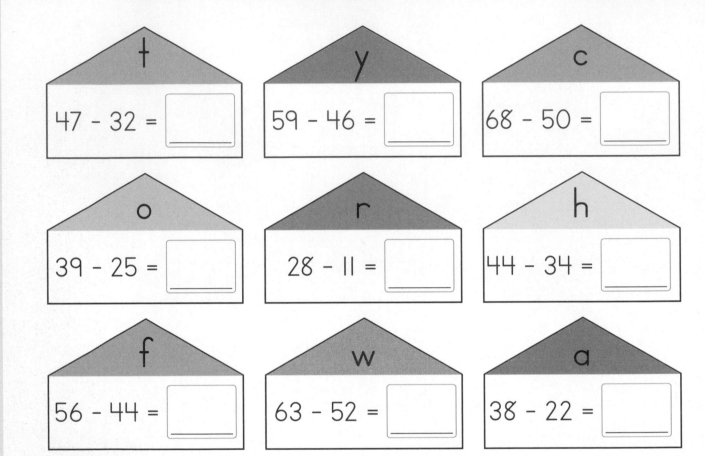

t: $47 - 32 =$ ☐

y: $59 - 46 =$ ☐

c: $68 - 50 =$ ☐

o: $39 - 25 =$ ☐

r: $28 - 11 =$ ☐

h: $44 - 34 =$ ☐

f: $56 - 44 =$ ☐

w: $63 - 52 =$ ☐

a: $38 - 22 =$ ☐

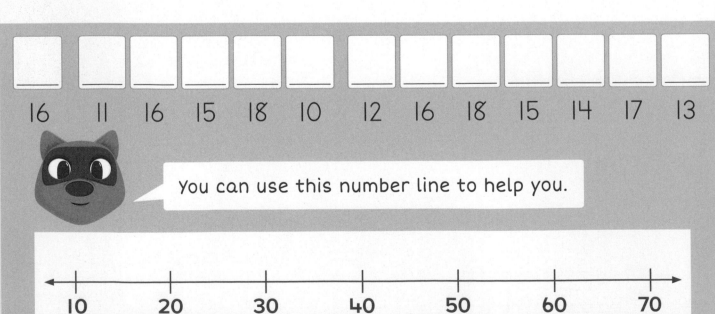

| 16 | 11 | 16 | 15 | 18 | 10 | 12 | 16 | 18 | 15 | 14 | 17 | 13 |

You can use this number line to help you.

10   20   30   40   50   60   70

I. Circle each polyhedron.

FROM 2.11.6

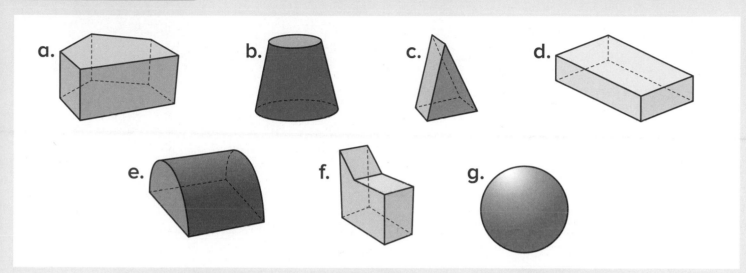

a.

b.

c.

d.

e.

f.

g.

2. Color one part of each shape red. Then write the fraction that is red.

FROM 2.12.3

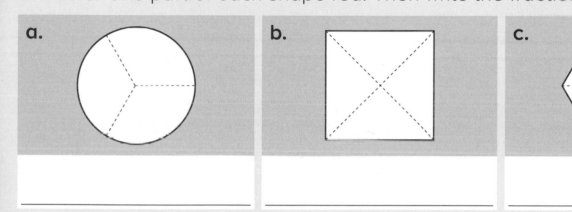

a.

b.

c.

_____

_____

_____

Look at these pictures of blocks. Write the matching number on the expander.

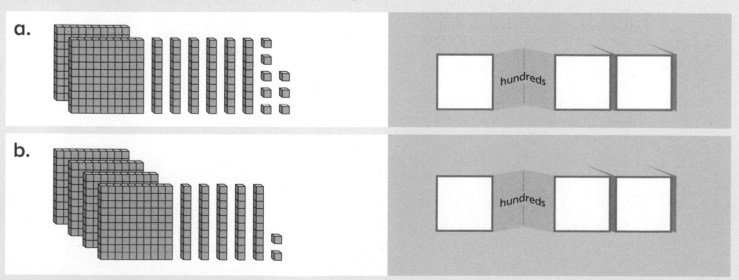

a.

hundreds

b.

hundreds

Step In

Look at this handprint.
How many whole squares are inside?

How many part squares are inside?
About how many squares are inside? How do you know?

Hugo drew the outline of his pencil case.

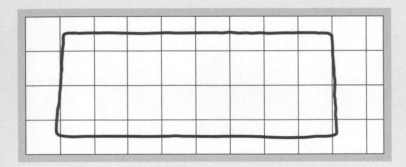

Write how many squares are inside.

About _____ squares

Imagine you had to figure out how much carpet is needed to cover the floor of a room. How could you figure it out?

Step Up

1. Write the number of squares that each picture covers.

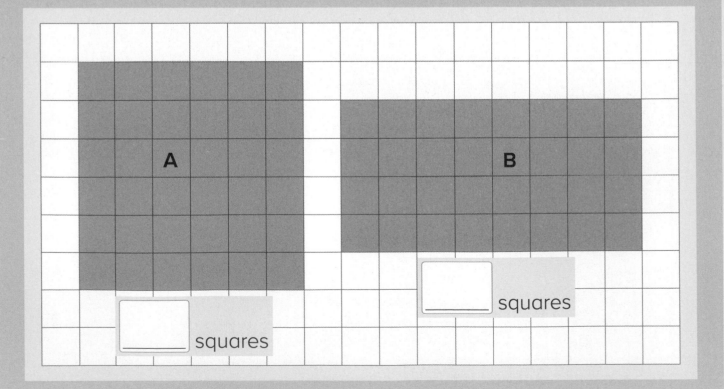

_____ squares

_____ squares

2. Look at the number of whole squares and part squares inside each picture. Write the total number of squares for each

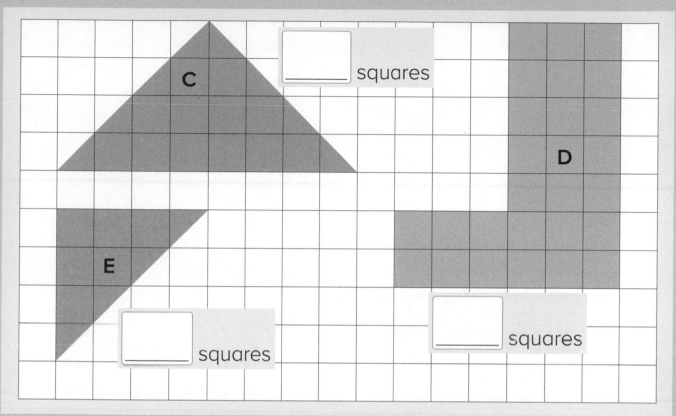

squares

3. Look at all the pictures in Questions 1 and 2.
Which picture covers the greatest number of squares? _____

1. This letter C has an area of 11 squares.
Color squares to show the first letter of your first name and last name.

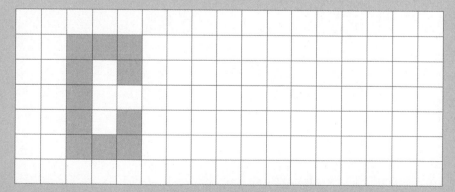

2. Write how many squares are in each letter.

a. first name _____ squares   b. last name _____ squares

Step In

What is a quick way to figure out the squares that the purple rectangle covers?

The purple rectangle covers 4 squares in each row. There are four rows, so that's 4, 8, 12, 16 squares in total.

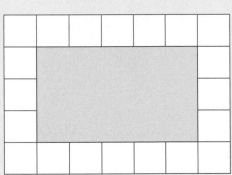

How could you use a similar method to figure out the number of squares that this yellow rectangle covers?

Step Up

1. Use a ruler to draw more rows and columns of squares. Then write the total number of squares in each rectangle.

a.

_____ squares

b.

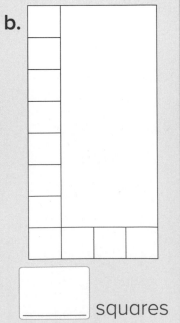

_____ squares

c.

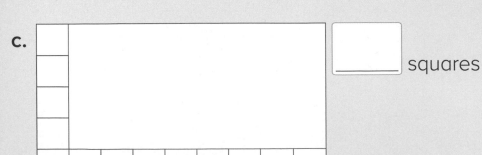

_____ squares

2. Write the number of squares that each rectangle covers.

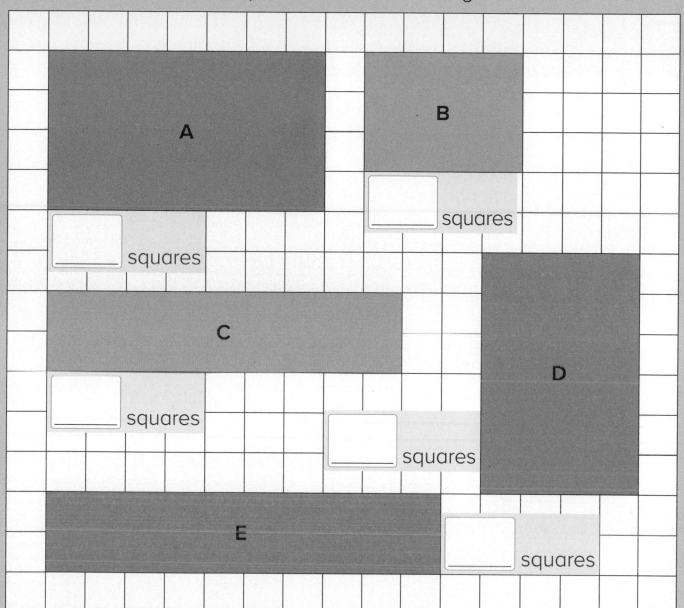

A _____ squares

B _____ squares

C _____ squares

_____ squares

D

E _____ squares

Step Ahead Color the ⬭ beside the thinking you could use to figure out the total number of squares that the rectangle covers.

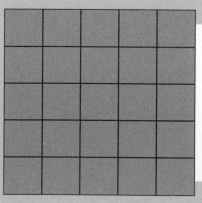

⬭ 5, 10, 15, 20. Twenty squares in total.

⬭ 6, 12, 18, 24. Twenty-four squares in total.

⬭ 5, 10, 15, 20, 25. Twenty-five squares in total.

© ORIGO Education

Think and Solve Some of the sides of this grid are covered.

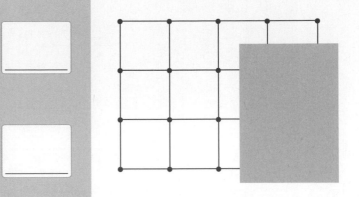

a. How many •——• are around the **outside** of the grid?

b. How many ☐ are inside the grid?

Words at Work   Does one-fourth always show the same quantity or amount? Write your thinking in words.

Ongoing Practice

1. Complete the chart. Use real objects to help you count the vertices, edges, and surfaces.

Object	Vertices	Straight edges	Curved edges	Flat surfaces	Curved surfaces
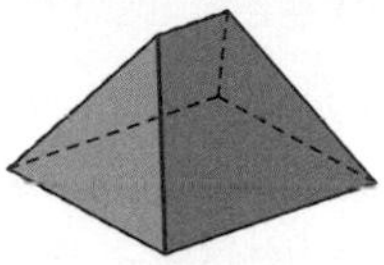	6				
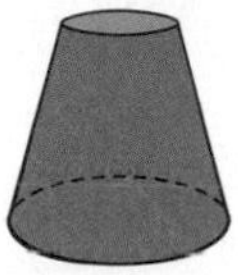		0			

FROM 2.11.8

2. Use a ruler to draw straight lines that show each shape split into the fractions shown. Make the splits different for each pair of shapes.

a. Halves

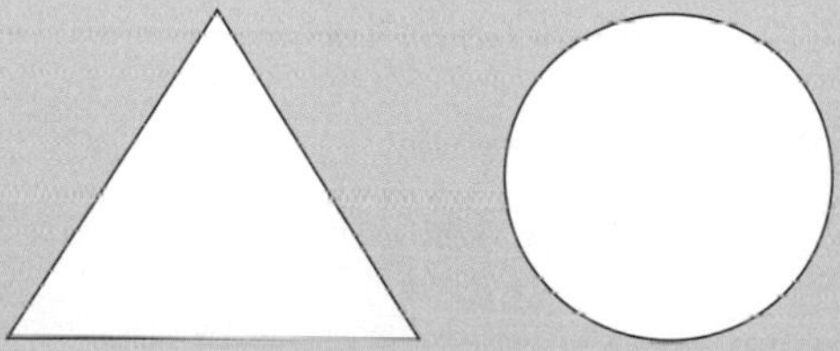

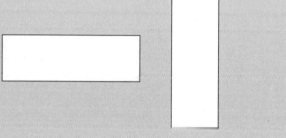

b. Thirds

FROM 2.12.6

Preparing for Next Year

Write the number on the expander in expanded form.

a.

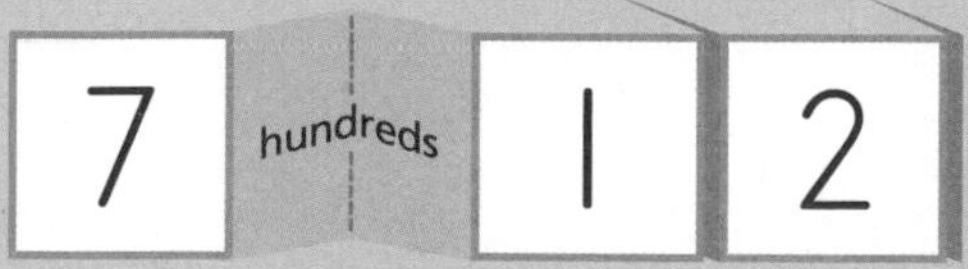
7
hundreds
1
2

________ + ________ + ______

b.

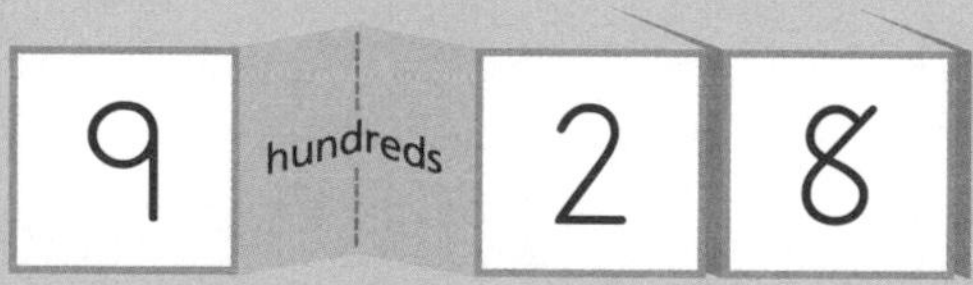
9
hundreds
2
8

________ + ________ + ______

c.

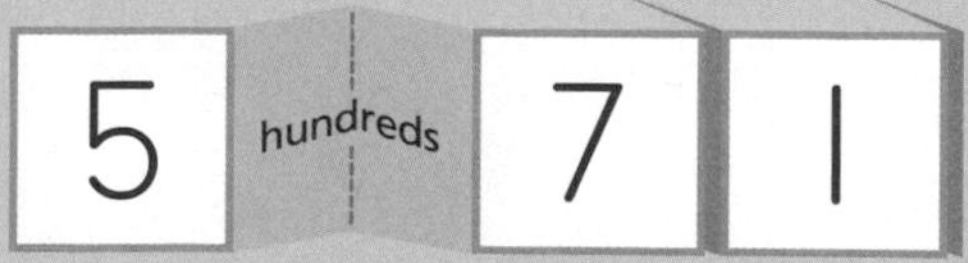
5
hundreds
7
1

________ + ________ + ______

d.

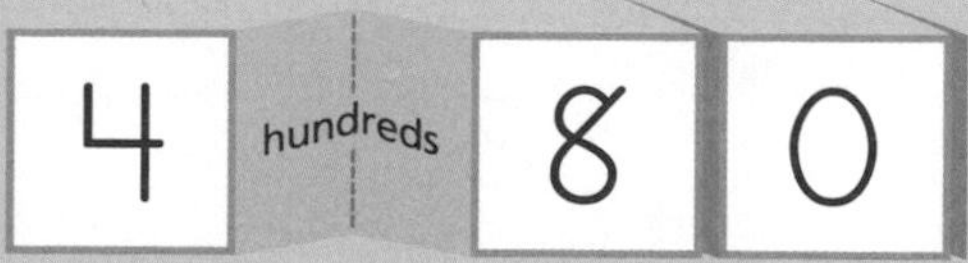
4
hundreds
8
0

________ + ________ + ______

Step In   What are some things you know about one pound?

What are some things that are measured in pounds?

What are some things that you think might weigh about one pound?

One of your shoes might weigh one pound.

A short way to write pound is lb. It comes from the Roman unit, libra.

A loaf of bread might weigh one pound.

Step Up   1. Look at the balance picture. Write **less than**, **equal to**, or **more than** to describe the mass of each object compared to one pound.

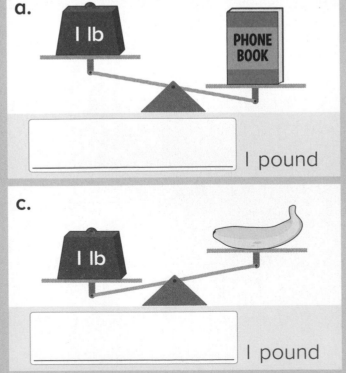

a. [I lb / PHONE BOOK]

_____ 1 pound

b. [bacon / I lb]

_____ 1 pound

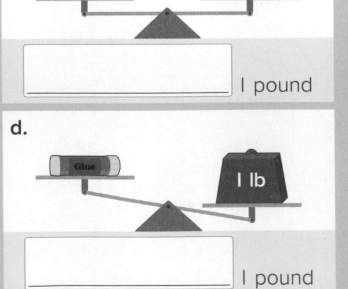

c. [I lb / banana]

_____ 1 pound

d. [Glue / I lb]

_____ 1 pound

2. Choose four objects in your classroom that you think each weigh one pound or more.

   a. Write the name of each object and estimate its mass.

Object	My estimate
A.	about _____ lb
B.	about _____ lb
C.	about _____ lb
D.	about _____ lb

   b. Your teacher will help you measure the mass of each object. Write each mass below.

Object A is about [ ] lb.   Object B is about [ ] lb.

Object C is about [ ] lb.   Object D is about [ ] lb.

   c. Which object had the greatest mass? _____

   d. Which object had the least mass? _____

Step Ahead   Write how much each object weighs.

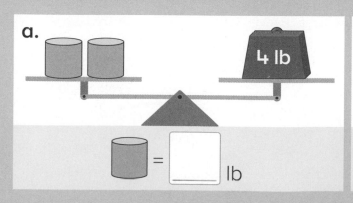

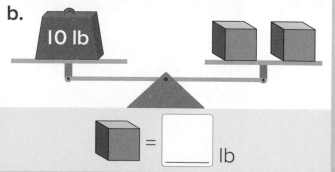

Step In

Objects in countries like France, Australia, and India, are not weighed in pounds.

Do you know what unit they use?

Where have you seen or heard about kilograms?

The short way to write kilograms is kg.

One kilogram is a little more than two pounds.
What are some things that you think weigh about one kilogram?

My water bottle when it is filled with water.

Some bags of rice or flour.

Pounds and kilograms are units of mass.
Mass is a measure of how heavy something is.

Step Up

I. Choose five objects in your classroom that you think each have a mass between 1 and 4 kilograms. Write them below.

Object A _____

Object B _____

Object C _____

Object D _____

Object E _____

© ORIGO Education

2. Your teacher will help you measure the mass of each object.
Write each mass in **kilograms** below.

Object A _____ kg   Object B _____ kg   Object C _____ kg

Object D _____ kg   Object E _____ kg

3. Your teacher will help you measure the mass of each object.
Write each mass in **pounds** below.

Object A _____ lb   Object B _____ lb   Object C _____ lb

Object D _____ lb   Object E _____ lb

4. Look at your answers for Questions 2 and 3. Why is the mass
of each object a greater number of pounds than kilograms?

_____
_____
_____

Step Ahead   Look at the first balance picture. Draw ■ to make
the second balance picture true.

Computation Practice

★ Complete the equations.
★ Then color each difference in the puzzle below.

68 – 53 = ☐

79 – 61 = ☐

46 – 32 = ☐

38 – 25 = ☐

57 – 40 = ☐

27 – 17 = ☐

75 – 63 = ☐

56 – 45 = ☐

69 – 50 = ☐

29 – 13 = ☐

Some differences appear more than once.

Ongoing Practice

I. Write the missing numbers.

a.

2 dimes is _____ ¢

3 nickels is _____ ¢

2 pennies is _____ ¢

The total is _____ ¢

b.

2 quarters is _____ ¢

2 dimes is _____ ¢

2 nickels is _____ ¢

The total is _____ ¢

2. Write **less than**, **equal to**, or **more than** to describe the mass of each object compared to one pound.

a.
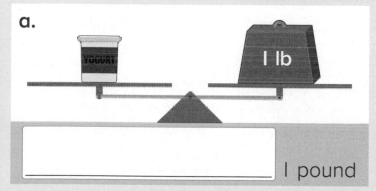

_____ I pound

b.
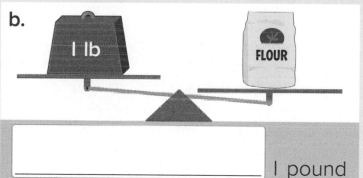

_____ I pound

Preparing for Next Year

Write the missing numbers.

a.

_____ rows of _____ is _____

_____ + _____ + _____ + _____ = _____

b.

_____ rows of _____ is _____

_____ + _____ + _____ = _____

Step In	All of these containers can be called cups.

If a recipe told you to use a cup of flour, which container would you use? Why? Would it make any difference? How do you know?

In recipes, the word cup is a unit of measure. Even though all cup measures hold the same amount, they can be different shapes.

Where have you seen or heard the words **pint** and **quart**?

> Cups, pints, and quarts are units of **capacity**.
>
> Capacity means how much a container can hold. So one pint of milk is the amount of milk that can fit in a one-pint bottle.

Step Up	1. Write **more** or **less** to show whether these containers would hold more than or less than one cup.

I cup

a.

_____

b.

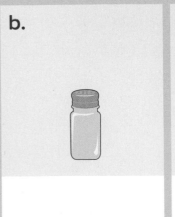

_____

c.

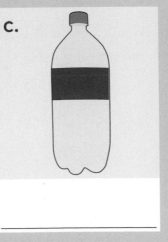

_____

2. Write **more** or **less** to show whether these containers would hold more than or less than one pint.

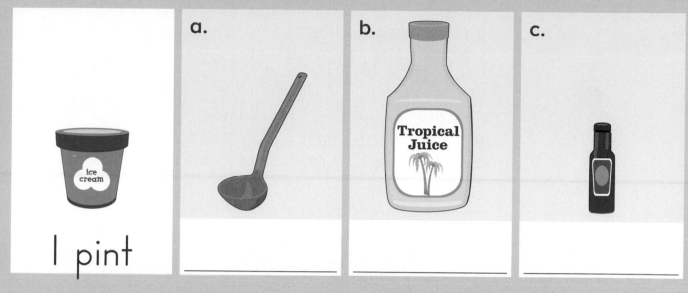

1 pint	a.	b. Tropical Juice	c.
	____	____	____

3. Write **more** or **less** to show whether these containers would hold more than or less than one quart.

1 quart	a. MILK	b.	c. ICE POP
	____	____	____

Step Ahead

Imagine a one-pint container can hold about 100 blocks. Color the containers that can hold closest to **half** a pint.

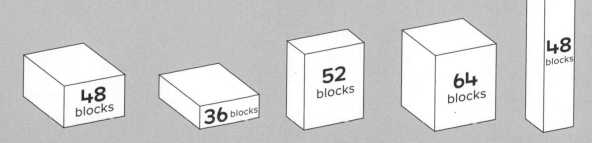

48 blocks   **36** blocks   **52** blocks   **64** blocks   **48** blocks

Step In   What do you know about liters?

We have a 3-liter bottle of cranberry juice at home.

Sometimes we buy soda that has 2 liters written on the bottle.

The liter is a metric unit of capacity that is used here and in other countries.

What are some containers that you think would hold about one liter?

Step Up   1.   Write **less than**, **about**, or **more than** to describe how much you think each container holds when compared to one liter.

Holds **exactly** 1 liter

a.

_____
1 liter

b.

_____
1 liter

c.

_____
1 liter

d.

_____
1 liter

e.

_____
1 liter

2. Your teacher will give you some containers to measure. Estimate the capacity of each container first. Use liters or half-liters. Then use the measuring containers to find the exact capacity.

Container	My estimate (liters)	Actual capacity (liters)
A		
B		
C		
D		
E		
F		

3. Which container had the **least** capacity?

4. Which container had the **greatest** capacity?

5. Which two containers together had a total capacity **greater than** 4 liters?

Step Ahead   Compare a container that holds 1 liter with a container that holds 1 quart. Then write what you notice.

Think and Solve Write how you can use the buckets to get **exactly** 24 scoops of water into the tub.

Buckets

A I scoop

B 3 scoops

C 5 scoops

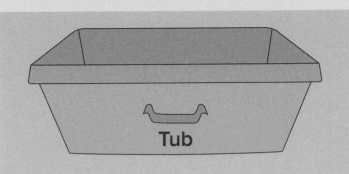
Tub

Words at Work Choose and write words from the list to complete these sentences. Some words are not used.

the same as	more than	kilogram	capacity	mass
less than	pounds	pints	liters	

a.

A horse would weigh _____ one pound.

b.

Kilograms and _____ are units of mass.

c.

One _____ is a little more than 2 pounds.

d.

_____ and _____ are units of capacity.

Ongoing Practice

1. Write the total.

The total is $ ____ and ____ ¢ .

2. Draw lines to match the containers to the amount you think they hold.

◄ one quart

◄ one cup

◄ one pint

Preparing for Next Year

Write a number story to match each picture.

a.

b.

© ORIGO Education

STUDENT GLOSSARY

3D object

A **three-dimensional (3D) object** has flat surfaces (e.g. a cube), curved surfaces (e.g. a sphere), or flat and curved surfaces (e.g. a cylinder or a cone).

A **polyhedron** is any closed 3D object that has four or more flat surfaces.

A **pyramid** is a polyhedron that has any polygon for a base. All the other surfaces joined to the base are triangles that meet at a point.

Addition

Addition is finding the total when two or more parts are known. When adding, another word for total is **sum**.

Part + Part = Total
2 + 3 = 5

Capacity

Capacity tells the amount a container can hold. For example, a cup **holds less** than a juice bottle.

A **liter** is a unit of capacity.
A **pint** is a unit of capacity.
A **quart** is a unit of capacity.

Common Fraction

Fractions describe equal parts of one whole.

 one-half    one-fourth

Even and odd numbers

Even numbers are whole numbers with 0, 2, 4, 6, or 8 in the ones place.
Odd numbers are whole numbers with 1, 3, 5, 7, or 9 in the ones place.

Fact family

An addition **fact family** includes an addition fact, its turnaround fact, and the two related subtraction facts.

$$4 + 2 = 6$$
$$2 + 4 = 6$$
$$6 - 4 = 2$$
$$6 - 2 = 4$$

STUDENT GLOSSARY

Graph

Different types of **graphs** can show data.

Vertical bar graph

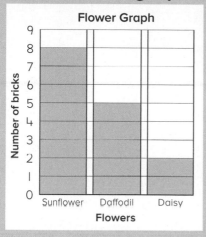

Horizontal bar graph

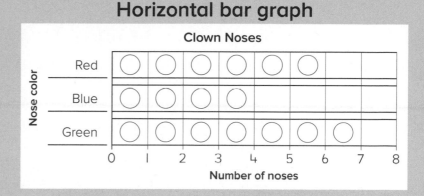

Line plot

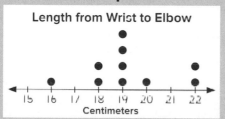

Picture graph

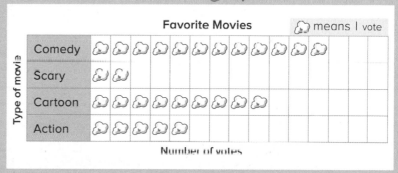

Hundred chart

A **hundred chart** makes it easy to see patterns with two-digit numbers.

Length

Length tells how long something is.

A **centimeter** is a unit of length. The short way to write centimeter is **cm**.

The **foot** is a unit of length. There are 3 feet in one yard. The short way to write foot is **ft**.

The **inch** is a unit of length. There are 12 inches in one foot. The short way to write inch is **in**.

A **meter** is a unit of length. The short way to write meter is **m**.

A **yard** is a unit of length. The short way to write yard is **yd**.

© ORIGO Education

STUDENT GLOSSARY

Mass

Mass tells the amount something weighs.
For example, a cat **weighs more** than a mouse.

A **kilogram** is a unit of mass. The short way to write kilogram is **kg**.

A **pound** is a unit of mass. The short way to write pound is **lb**.

Mental computation strategies for addition

Strategies you can use to figure out a mathematical problem in your head.

Count-on *See* 3 + 8 *think* 8 + 1 + 1 + 1
       See 58 + 24 *think* 58 + 10 + 10 + 4

Doubles   *See* 7 + 7 *think* double 7
       See 25 + 26 *think* double 25 plus 1 more
       See 35 + 37 *think* double 35 plus 2 more

Make-ten   *See* 9 + 4 *think* 9 + 1 + 3
       See 38 + 14 *think* 38 + 2 + 12

Place value *See* 32 + 27 *think* 32 + 20 + 7

Mental computation strategies for subtraction

Strategies you can use to figure out a mathematical problem in your head.

Count-back *See* 9 − 2 *think* 9 − 1 − 1
        See 26 − 20 *think* 26 − 10 − 10

Think addition *See* 17 − 9 *think* 9 + 8 = 17 so 17 − 9 = 8

Multiplication

Multiplication is used to find the total number of objects in an array, or in a number of equal groups.

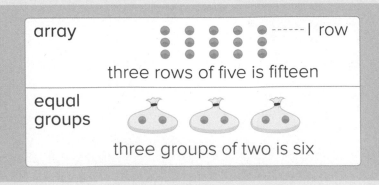

array   ------ I row

three rows of five is fifteen

equal groups

three groups of two is six

STUDENT GLOSSARY

Number facts

Addition facts are equations that add two one-digit numbers.
For example: $2 + 3 = 5$ or $3 = 1 + 2$

Subtraction facts are subtraction equations related
to the addition facts above. For example: $5 - 2 = 3$ or $3 - 2 = 1$

Number line

A **number line** shows the position
of a number. The number line can
be used to show addition and subtraction.

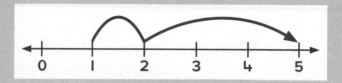

Polygon

A **polygon** is any closed 2D shape
that has three or more straight sides
(e.g. triangle, quadrilateral, pentagon, and hexagon).

Subtraction

Subtraction is finding a part when
the total and one part are known.

$$\textbf{Total} - \textbf{Part} = \textbf{Part}$$
$$5 \ - \ 2 \ = \ 3$$
$$\textbf{Part} + \underline{} = \textbf{Total}$$
$$2 \ + \underline{} = \ 5$$

Turnaround fact

Each addition fact has a related **turnaround fact**. (This is also known as the
Commutative Property.) For example: $2 + 7 = 9$ and $7 + 2 = 9$

© ORIGO Education

TEACHER INDEX

© ORIGO Education

TEACHER INDEX

TEACHER INDEX

© ORIGO Education